BOOK CARD

Other books by Simon Hartley:

Hartley, S. (2012). *How To Shine: Insights into unlocking your potential from proven winners*. Capstone.

Hartley, S. (2013). *Two Lengths of the Pool. HLS* Publishing Solutions.

Hartley, S. (2014). *Could I Do That?* Capstone.

Hartley, S. (2014). *How To Herd Cats: Leading a Team of Independent Thinkers*. CreateSpace.

Hartley, S. (2016). *Stronger Together: How Great Teams Work.* Piatkus.

Haryley, S. (2016). *How to Develop Character: Beyond Skills, Knowledge and Personality*. CreateSpace.

MASTER

MENTAL TOUGHNESS

SIMON HARTLEY

be world class

Let's Tell YouR Story Publishing
London

COPYRIGHT

CONTENTS

FOREWORD:
DINO TARTAGLIA, CO-FOUNDER OF SUCCESS ENGINEERS

In Nicomachean ethics, Aristotle remarks that "The prudent man strives for freedom from pain, not for pleasure."

In this quick study, Simon Hartley has distilled decades of insight not just into what makes the best in the world truly 'world class', but also into how we can use this understanding to allow us to master mental toughness.

Interestingly, Simon doesn't focus on moving us away from pain but, rather, he focuses on unlocking and realising our full potential – in truly developing all that we are. In becoming better in the areas of our life that really matter to us, through mastering and synthesising together all of the components of mental toughness. In doing so, we do, indeed, "strive for freedom from pain" as we become more resilient and, above all, more self-effacing.

Most of the concepts in the five-stage process he discusses in his method are simple bridges that enable us to walk from where we are to where we wish to be, making this accessible to everyone who seeks self-improvement.

If you've been looking for a touchstone for personal development, congratulations! You've finally found what you seek.

With a world class ability to show you and me how to become more confident, more focused, more motivated...better and more resilient version of who we are...Simon Hartley's experience, thinking and insights combine to create that touchstone by which all personal development should be assessed.

I've had the great pleasure and the enormous privilege of working with him over many years. I've watched the man grow from a talented Sports Psych into a world-class coach, insightful critical thinker, highly effective communicator and sought-after keynote speaker and author. This book distils all of that wisdom and experience into an easy-to-absorb, bite-sized read.

This is the end of your search and the beginning of your journey to fulfilling your true potential.

Master Mental Toughness gives you a solid foundation on which you can build everything you ever wanted.

Read, enjoy, absorb and then...*implement*...and everything will change for you.

Dino Tartaglia
Warsaw, 2018
www.successengineers.co.uk

HI, I'M SIMON

The purpose of this book is really simple. It exists to help you develop mental toughness in yourself and others. For a little over 20 years now, I've been working with highly successful people. Many of them are world class performers in their field. It won't surprise you to know that one of the key characteristics they all share is... mental toughness. It's one of those critical characteristics that underpins success. I suspect that doesn't come as a huge surprise to you.

But the question is...

HOW CAN WE DEVELOP MENTAL TOUGHNESS?

As a sport psychology consultant and world class performance coach, I've spent over 20 years developing mental toughness in my clients. As a result, many of them have achieved extreme success. Some have broken world records, won world championships and gained Olympic medals. Others have grown multi-million-pound businesses or become world leaders in their field.

I know how critical mental toughness is to success. And I want to be successful too. So, I asked myself...

DO I HAVE THE MENTAL TOUGHNESS I NEED?

Bizarre as this might sound, although I've helped countless others to become mentally tough, it was something I struggled with. I knew that I would often back-off or quit when things got really tough. To be honest, I'd never pushed myself hard enough to find my true limit either.

So, I challenged myself.

I know how to develop it in others.

HOW CAN I DEVELOP IT IN MYSELF?

Through this book I will share two elements, that will help you develop mental toughness.

I'll share a five-stage process that I've used to help my clients achieve their success.

And, I'll share my personal experiences of developing mental toughness in myself.

When you read this book, you'll notice that I give a few examples from my work as a sport psychology consultant. I'll share some case studies from elite athletes and sports teams. You'll see the word "athlete" appear a few times. However, this is not "sports thinking". This is human thinking! It is not restricted to sport or athletic endeavours. It applies equally to all of us... no matter what we do.

This has been an incredibly powerful journey for me; both professionally and personally.

My hope is that this little book can also help you develop the mental toughness you need, so that you can achieve the success you desire.

INTRODUCTION

WHY DO WE NEED MENTAL TOUGHNESS?

Arguably, to be successful, we need a healthy dose of mental toughness. I have seen first-hand evidence of this in my own work with world-class athletes. Whilst researching my second book, *How To Shine*[1] I also interviewed world-class performers in a diverse range of disciplines outside of sport, to find out what differentiates them from their peers. It seems mental toughness is a key factor in the success of a chef with multiple Michelin stars, a world-class mountaineer, a world barista champion, a record-breaking polar explorer, the head of a world-renowned science organisation and special forces personnel.

Mental toughness allows these people to push themselves and extend their limits. It enables them to thrive in adversity. Their mental toughness drives them to take on those challenges that their peers back away from. It allows them to constantly improve their performance by trying and failing! Perhaps more importantly, it also enables them to ask those uncomfortable, searching, questions and find the difficult answers.

If we wish to develop mental toughness ourselves, it makes sense to begin by understanding what it is...and is not!

STAGES OF MENTAL TOUGHNESS

Through this book, I will share a step-by-step process to build mental strength. This not only gives you the theory, but also a practical way to translate it into your life.

The five stages are:

- Understanding mental toughness
- Consistent optimal performance
- Accountability and responsibility
- Entering "the discomfort zone"
- Toughness – resilience, tenacity and composure

This book is a practical guide. My aim is to give you strategies, methods and tools that you can take away and use in your own life. Each stage is designed to give you practical examples from world class performers and help you understand how to apply these principles yourself.

When I kick-off workshops, I often say, "If you leave here saying it's been interesting, or enjoyable, we've missed a trick. To gain the true value from this we have to take it away, use it and apply it. Only then do we gain the real value from it". So, please don't just read this book. Please use what you learn, apply it and extract the real power from it.

As Sir Edmund Hillary once said:

> "It is not the mountain we conquer but ourselves"

STAGE ONE: UNDERSTANDING MENTAL TOUGHNESS

WHAT IS MENTAL TOUGHNESS?

Here are a few thoughts...

> *"Mental toughness is the ability to get fuel from an empty tank."*
> **Anon**

> *"It's hard to beat a person who never gives up."*
> **Babe Ruth, major league baseball player**

> *"Mental toughness is a state of mind – you could call it 'character in action'"*
> **Vince Lombardi, American football coach**

> *"Mental toughness is the ability to face adversity, failure and negative events without a loss of effort, attitude and enthusiasm"*
> **Anon (probably based on Churchill's famous quote)**

> *"To me, football is so much about mental toughness; it's digging deep... it's doing whatever you need to do to help the team win."*
> **Tom Brady, American football player**

To be honest, if you do a quick Google search you'll find hundreds more. You'll probably find some you like more than these. Quotes are fine.

To a certain extent, they might give us an insight into mental toughness. But, they're not definitions.

More importantly, they don't necessarily help us to understand mental toughness from our own experience either.

What do the clever folk think?

Sport psychology researcher, Dr. Michael Sheard[2], has investigated this phenomenon we call 'mental toughness'. He also acknowledges how important it is to the success of athletes and sports teams. In fact, Dr. Sheard describes it as "the stuff of champions"; in his words "the courage to stand tall in the face of adversity and refuse to be intimidated".

Jon Hammermeister[3] (a performance psychologist from the US Army) recognises that some of the skills associated with mental toughness include the ability to:

- Be self-motivated
- Maintain confidence
- Focus under pressure
- Be in control of emotions
- Consistently perform close to one's potential

Whilst that's useful information, it doesn't necessarily help us to identify mentally tough individuals when we see them. To make it more real:

- How would you know a mentally tough person if you saw one?
- What traits would they exhibit?
- What characteristics would you see?
- How would they behave?
- What would they say?

To truly understand mental toughness, we need to know what it is... and is not!

We need to understand when we're seeing true mental toughness and when we're not. Interestingly, those who beat their chests and shout a lot are often not displaying mental toughness at all.

We need to get under the skin; beyond the dictionary definitions. If we want to develop mental toughness, we need to know what it looks like, sounds like, thinks like and behaves like. And, we need to understand it from a personal, experiential, perspective.

Once we understand what mental toughness really is, we can start to develop it.

Even after years of studying the sport psychology research and the textbooks, my understanding of mental toughness was quite vague. It was almost like I 'sort of' understood it; like seeing something that's blurred... through a lens that isn't focused.

So, here's an exercise to help bring this all into focus!

FOCUSING ON YOUR MENTAL TOUGHNESS

- Who do you know that is mentally tough?
- When have you displayed mental toughness yourself?
- What does mental toughness look like, sound like, think like and act like?
- What do you notice about people who are genuinely displaying mental toughness?
- How do they respond to the challenges they're facing?
- What do they say?
- What do they do?

Think of a time when you were at your toughest.

- How were you thinking?
- What kinds of thoughts occupied your mind?
- What was the conversation between your ears?
- How did you feel?

Now, think of a time when you were not so mentally tough?

- How were you thinking?
- What kinds of thoughts occupied your mind?
- What was the conversation between your ears?
- How did you feel?

It is definitely worth taking some time out and really thinking about these questions, writing down your answers and really reflecting on them. If you want to change anything in your life, awareness is a powerful ingredient!

NOTES

MY OWN EXPERIENCES

In my work as a sport psychology consultant and performance coach, I have been fascinated by the concept of mental toughness. I have seen many athletes and teams who have crumbled when they've hit tough challenges. Some teams imploded at crucial times during a game, or during a season. Some panicked when they went behind. They seemed to throw their game plan out of the window when they were questioned.

For many years, I defined mental toughness as the ability to stick to the game plan; no matter what! Obviously, 'the game plan' needs to be flexible and adaptable. However, I would argue that we should not abandon it completely and start panicking at the first sign of trouble.

I have also seen many athletes that seem to shrivel up when they're exposed to criticism. It is hard for some to take; especially if that criticism is very vocal and comes from 40,000 angry fans on a Saturday afternoon. In fact, whilst working in an English Premier League football club a number of years ago, our coaching staff developed a saying...

"When the going gets tough, the tough hide under the treatment table".

We used to see the number of injuries rise (and take longer to heal) when the team was struggling, and the players were being booed by the fans. The players were actually using the treatment room to escape! Interestingly, our captain (who did the shouting and fist waving) was the most regular visitor to the treatment room if we lost at home. Of course, our problem wasn't bruised bodies; it was bruised egos.

MENTAL TOUGHNESS CLUES

Michael Sheard[2] identifies a number of traits that he associates with mentally tough athletes. These include:

- Winning mentality
- Work ethic
- Self-confidence
- Motivation
- Attitude control
- Positive energy

When I work with athletes, I notice a group of traits that inform me about their mental toughness.

1. Athletes who consistently perform at their best in adverse conditions.

Mentally tough athletes tend to be focused, confident and motivated, whatever the situation. Every athlete experiences their peaks and troughs, whether that is through injury, lack of form, de-selection, a run of poor results, or whatever. Every athlete has been in situations where the chips are down, and they have their backs to the wall. Mentally tough athletes tend to apply themselves consistently, whether they are on a high, or at the bottom of the deepest low. I often say to athletes,

"I'm not that interested how good you are on a great day. I want to know what you're like on the shitty days."

2. Athletes who come back stronger from set-backs.

Athletes with mental strength tend to display 'bounce-back ability'. I have come to realise that truly great athletes seem to experience the same amount of 'good luck' and 'bad luck' as everyone else. However, their response to their 'luck' is normally different. When they experience setbacks, mentally tough athletes knuckle down, apply themselves, learn as much as they possibly can from the experience and grow from it. As a result, they tend to come back stronger.

3. Athletes who are composed in 'pressurised situations'.

When athletes perceive that they are under pressure, some will panic. Sometimes the game plan flies out of the window and they start to make strange decisions and unforced errors. Mentally tough athletes, however, tend to have the ability to remain composed. They tend not to panic. They stay on task, keep focused and stick to the game plan. When they make mistakes, they simply focus back onto the task in hand and execute their skills.

4. Athletes who actively seek out, and thrive in, their 'discomfort zone'.

Some athletes will respond well if they are pushed outside of their comfort zones. Truly great athletes go a step further. They actively seek out opportunities to push themselves into their discomfort zone. The world-class athletes that I've worked with will say that the alarm bells start ringing when they become comfortable. These people relish the challenge and go looking for it!

5. Athletes who push to their limit, not just the point of discomfort.

Most people stop when things become uncomfortable. Although you tend think of this in a physical sense (i.e. the point you become tired or feel physical pain), this concept extends to other limits too. Some people give up when they've tried a new skill a few times and it hasn't worked perfectly. They don't like the feeling of 'failing' because it is uncomfortable. Other people keep going and keep failing, until they get it right. They don't stop at the point where it becomes uncomfortable; they stop when they hit their limit.

6. **Athletes who are self-critical and seek critical feedback from others.**

Some people are uncomfortable with criticism. Others will listen, take criticism on board and acknowledge it. The better athletes will recognise that it is a gift and use it to its fullest extent. The world-class performers that I've met actually seek out critical feedback and then squeeze every possible ounce of benefit from it. To them, critical feedback is like oxygen. It fuels their development. Without it they know they cannot grow.

EXTREME MENTAL TOUGHNESS

Over the years I have witnessed many athletes and teams who displayed extreme mental toughness. I worked with incredibly tough individuals; such as mountaineers, polar explorers, adventure racers, extreme athletes and special-forces personnel. These people conquer some phenomenal challenges.

Mountaineer, Alan Hinkes, is one of around a dozen people who have reached the summit of all fourteen of the world's 8000+ meter peaks. On one occasion he found himself in a nightmare situation at the peak of the world's third highest mountain. He was 8500 meters above sea level, on his own, in the dark and in the middle of a blizzard. In his words, he thought he was going to die. Alan's mental toughness enabled him to focus on the job in hand and get himself off the mountain!

Polar explorer, Ben Saunders, has faced similar dangers in his solo treks in the Arctic when exhausted, starving hungry, frostbitten and under attack from a polar bear.

World-record breaking ultra-runner, Andy McMenemy, completed 66 ultra-marathons in 66 days. He injured his Achilles tendon on day two and was admitted to hospital on day 26 with a suspected fractured shin. Amazingly, he got up on day 27 and ran an ultra-marathon.

These are all extreme displays of mental toughness!

In fact, after watching some truly tough people and listening to their stories, I extended my definition to include....

> *"the ability to keep going and not give up, even when every fibre of your being screams at you to stop".*

But not all of us will be at the top of 8,000m high mountains, or crossing the Arctic Ocean, or running through a gun battle. So, how would you notice mental toughness outside of those extreme conditions?

What would it look like in a sports team, for example?

Is the toughest individual the loudest? Are they the one who runs out of the dressing room screaming? Are they the one who is most physically dominant?

Or... are they the ones who will push themselves the hardest? Are they willing to enter their discomfort zone? Are they the people that will venture into the unknown and take on new challenges? Perhaps, the toughest are those that take complete responsibility for their performance at all times.

Of course, pushing ourselves to our limits, seeking our discomfort zone, venturing into the unknown, taking on new challenges and taking complete responsibility are features of toughness in any walk of life; not just sport.

MENTALLY TOUGH ATHLETES

In 2006, I worked with a Team GB Olympic swimmer called Chris Cook, as he prepared for the final of a major world event. He was waiting in the 'call room' with the other seven finalists. One of them, an Australian, came up to Chris and rubbed his knuckle on Chris' head. He started trying to intimidate Chris verbally and physically, in an attempt to undermine Chris' confidence. Chris sat, looked at him and smiled. He didn't say a word in response because he didn't need to.

Chris knew that the Australian was in trouble. Why did the Australian feel the need to intimidate Chris? Did he not think he could win the race on his own merit? Did he have to pull Chris back, in order to stand a chance of beating him? Interestingly, Dr. Michael Sheard[2] referred to 'a refusal to be intimidated', in his description of mental toughness. This is not the same as feeling the need to intimidate others!

Sometimes fear can be dressed up as toughness. Bravado tends to be a façade: a form of 'fake toughness'. In fact, I would suggest that bravado is often a sign of weakness rather than strength.

Chris knew that his job was simple. He had to swim two lengths of that swimming pool as quickly as he could. He'd worked incredibly hard in training and could not have been better prepared. He'd overcome considerable adversity to get there, which gave him a deep sense of confidence in his own ability. All he had to do now was to swim two lengths of the pool. If Chris swam quicker than everyone else, he'd win. If someone else swam faster than him, they'd win. Chris knew if he simply swam as quickly as he could, he'd done his job. It doesn't get any more complicated than that.

If you want to know what mental toughness looks like, you can learn a lot from this example. The tough athlete is not the one trying to dominate or intimidate his opponent. The tougher of the two is the one who sat calmly, smiled and looked his opponent in the eye. He's also the one that remained completely focused on his job and refused to be distracted from it. I doubt you'll be surprised when I tell you that Chris won the gold medal that day! This is all very well, but it doesn't answer the burning question.

HOW DO YOU DEVELOP MENTAL TOUGHNESS?

In my experience mental toughness often develops by chance, rather than by design. For example, people can become tough as a result of their environment. Sometimes they are in an intensely competitive environment. To survive and thrive in those surroundings, they have to develop toughness. Through his studies of the world's sporting 'Gold Mines', Rasmus Ankersen[4] noted that in many cases fierce competition gives rise to mentally tough athletes.

To succeed in the incredibly competitive environment, athletes were forced to become tough. If you want to become a successful female golfer in South Korea, or a world-class female tennis player in Russia, or a distance-runner in Kenya, you have to be tough enough to beat the thousands of others hoping to pip you to the dream. In Rasmus' words, there is a tiny percentage who 'pass through the eye of the needle'. The intensity of the training and competition dictates that only the toughest will make it.

In Jamaica, promising athletes attend the school athletics championships, "The Champs". It is designed to be a 'high pressure' cauldron for the young athletes. 'The Champs' is the focus of the entire nation. The stadium is packed with 30,000 people. It is on television and on the radio. Everyone is watching.

The thinking is simple. If a junior athlete can perform at 'The Champs', they'll be able to perform anywhere.

However, you cannot rely on the world around you to make us tough. It is rare that we will find ourselves in an extreme environment that demands mental toughness from us. Our modern

Western world is often too comfortable. Therefore, if we want to develop mental toughness, we need to know how to cultivate it. Personally, I would argue that mental toughness should not be left to chance. That is why this book provides the tools and resources to help you develop mental toughness deliberately and intentionally.

'Master mental toughness' is a five-stage program. Think of it like stairs in a staircase. Each of the stages needs to be understood and mastered because it underpins the next.

This is Stage 1 – understanding mental toughness. It helps to know:

- What it looks like, sounds like, thinks like and acts like
- How we recognise it when we see it.
- How we detect the subtle signs that tell us that we are becoming tougher.

Simply understanding what toughness looks like can help us to develop it.

Here's a tool that might help. It's called, 'The Mental Toughness Matrix'. I've used the mental toughness matrix to help assess and develop toughness in elite and professional sport, education, the military and the world of business.

THE MENTAL TOUGHNESS MATRIX

The Mental Toughness Matrix helps us assess toughness according to six key characteristics. For each of the characteristics, there is a description of what we might see and hear from people who are "tough", "not so tough" and three points in between...

TRAIT	NOT SO TOUGH				TOUGH
Consistency in Adverse Conditions	Can be significantly affected by relatively small adverse events. Performances tend to follow changes in the situation.	Performance can be affected by relatively minor adverse conditions but the fluctuation is less significant.	Resistant to the more minor adverse conditions, but can be affected by moderate of more extreme situations.	Performance is generally stable, but can be affected by extreme adversity. However, performance swings are likely to be smaller.	Maintains focus, consistently delivers the processes with high quality execution in any situation.
Response to Set-Backs	Tends to experience significant knocks when they encounter set-backs. Normally emerges weaker as a result. Set-backs can be catastrophic.	Set-backs tend to leave 'scars'. Normally, the person does not return from the event as strongly. They tend to view set-backs as negative.	Tends not to be knocked by set-backs and normally comes back to a point of parity from any event.	Can gain from and learn from set-backs, finding opportunities that can give them some advantage.	Uses set-backs as an opportunity to strengthen. As a result they consistently emerge stronger from an event.
Composure Under Pressure	Often perceives 'pressure' in a situation and tends to crumble – makes strange decisions, abandons the game plan, panics and makes significant errors.	Becomes erratic and prone to errors when situations turn against them or if they perceive they are 'under pressure'.	Can become erratic or prone to errors in situations that they perceive to be 'highly pressurised'.	May become slightly more conservative, or take more risks in situations they perceive as 'highly pressurised'.	Consistent in their decision making, adherence to the game plan, focus and execution, in any situation.

Appetite for Discomfort Zone	Actively avoids their discomfort zone and consciously backs away from challenges that push them.	Will occasionally enter their discomfort zone for short periods if the situation demands.	Will push into their discomfort zone when the need demands, but will normally only remain there as long as the demand remains.	Will choose to operate on the edge of their comfort / discomfort zone regularly, and take more significant strides into discomfort occasionally.	Actively seeks opportunities to take significant steps into their discomfort zone.
Willingness to The Limit	Tends to give up before things become uncomfortable. Has no idea where their true limit is.	Normally gives up at the point of mild discomfort or early experiences of discomfort.	Will endure discomfort on a needs basis, but tends not to endure significant discomfort for extended periods.	Will endure significant discomfort for extended periods and operate close to their true limits.	Will push it until breaking point so that they know the true limit, and then operate very close to the limit regularly.
Perception of Critical Feedback	Struggles to accept criticism and tends to ignore it.	Will accept some critical feedback, often begrudgingly, and occasionally acts upon it.	Accepts critical feedback comfortably and often uses it.	Readily accepts and uses critical feedback regularly, and views it as an opportunity to improve.	Actively seeks critical feedback, is proactively self-critical and works to get the maximum benefit from it.

Importantly, the mental toughness matrix also shows the journey from "not so tough" to "tough"; from left to right through the matrix. These are the changes we see, hear and feel as we become tougher. They give us a way of understanding our progress and seeing the next change we can make on our journey towards becoming mentally tough.

WHERE ARE YOU ON THE MENTAL TOUGHNESS MATRIX?

Take a moment. Right now...

- What do you typically see and hear from yourself in each of these six characteristics?
- What's your next step?
- How can you ensure you take that next step towards "tough"?

STAGE TWO: CONSISTENT OPTIMAL PERFORMANCE

What's the difference between your best performance, and your worst performance? Many people find that their performance fluctuates wildly from their best day to their worst. However, the very best performers find a way to perform close to their best in any situation.

How do they do that?

Let's take a deeper look!

THE FOUNDATION

If you look back at what mental toughness is, you see phrases like:

- "the ability to be self-motivated"
- "maintain confidence and focus under pressure"
- "be in control of emotions"
- "consistently perform close to our potential"

It stands to reason that anyone who wants to maintain confidence under pressure, must first be able to control their own confidence. Equally, if you wish to remain focused under pressure: arguably you need to know how to hone your focus.

To keep going, even when you're tempted to quit, you need to master your motivation! In order to consistently perform close to our potential, you need to know how to engineer your mind and emotions to give you consistent optimal performance.

Whenever we look at the requirements of mental toughness, or indeed the requirements of a great mental game, we see the same key components:

- Focus
- Confidence
- Motivation

These three elements are fundamental to developing a great mental game, and ultimately to developing mental toughness. They are also vital, if we want to perform in adversity.

PERFORMING CONSISTENTLY

You may remember that 'consistency in adverse conditions' is one of the key elements in the mental toughness matrix. It also shows what we're likely to see and hear from people who are 'not so tough' (on the left-hand side) to 'tough' (right-hand side).

'Not so tough' players are vulnerable to distractions whilst the tougher players are completely focused on the task at hand and able to consistently deliver; regardless of the situation. It also shows there is a journey, from left to right.

Therefore, you can develop from 'not so tough' to 'tough', by following this path.

Consistency in Adverse Conditions	Can be significantly affected by relatively small adverse events. Performances tend to follow changes in the situation.	Performance can be affected by relatively minor adverse conditions but the fluctuation is less significant.	Resistant to the more minor adverse conditions, but can be affected by moderate of more extreme situations.	Performance is generally stable, but can be affected by extreme adversity. However, performance swings are likely to be smaller.	Maintains focus, consistently delivers the processes with high quality execution in any situation.
	➡	➡	➡	➡	

Consistency is your ability to perform at your best, regardless of the situation. It is foundational; part of the bedrock on which mental toughness is built. To perform at your best in any situation, you need to be able to take complete control over your thoughts and feelings. You need to be able to master and control our focus, confidence and motivation. Critically, these skills also underpin your ability to perform under 'pressure'.

WORKINGS OF THE HUMAN MIND

Several years ago, I was working with a group of senior partners in a highly prestigious UK business, helping them to maximise their personal performance and the performance of the people around them. I explained that focus, confidence and motivation were the foundation of our mental game. During one of the sessions I was asked:

> "So, which is most important then; confidence, motivation or focus?"

To be honest, I had never been asked the question before, so I had to stop and think for a minute. My brain tends to work in pictures and images. The image that entered my mind was that of a Formula One (F1) car. I explained that there are many key components in the car, all of which depend on each other. Having one on its own will not win you the race. It is the same with our mind. Crucially, confidence, motivation and focus work together. The F1 car as a fantastic analogy for this.

Imagine the F1 car. It has an incredibly powerful and finely tuned engine. Obviously, to produce the immense speeds required to win a race, you need a powerful engine. However, a powerful engine alone will not win the race. A Dragster has a powerful engine, but it would not win the Monaco Grand Prix.

Power is not the only quality that the car needs to possess. If we want to win a race, our F1 car also requires manoeuvrability.

Formula One races are not run on straight tracks. Therefore, F1 cars need to have a state-of-the-art steering system to successfully navigate the course at high speed. As we all know, even these two components are not enough to win. In fact, even if we went through every nut and bolt in the car we would still not find all the components required. To win a race, we need elements that lie outside the body of the car as well. Probably the most obvious is the driver.

Arguably the driver is one of the most vital factors. If we had the best engine on earth, the number one steering system and the finest nuts and bolts money could buy, we won't win the race with a timid driver who gets scared driving over 30 mph.

This talk of F1 cars is all well and good, but how does it relate to our trio of confidence, motivation and focus? This is how I see it:

- Motivation is the engine. It is sometimes known as `drive'. It will provide us with the power and energy that we need.
- Focus is our steering system. Motivation alone is not enough. If our motivation is undirected, we won't achieve our goals. It is very easy to be a motivated, energetic fool who runs around doing all sorts of interesting things that never produce an outcome. I suspect this is something we are all guilty of occasionally.
- Confidence is our driver. Will the driver push himself and the car to the limits of its capacity, or back off a little at the crucial moments? Will the driver have enough confidence in the game plan to bide his time

and only strike at exactly the right moment, or will he force a move that isn't there and spin off? Can the driver hold his nerve at crucial points in the race, or will he crack?

Maybe that's a long-winded way of saying you need all three. However, it is a lot more than that. It shows that these three elements are dependent on each other and that there is an interaction between them. They are inter-dependent. They all impact on each other. If they were colours, they would merge together as a spectrum rather than being individual blobs on a page.

If you look at the relationship between the three more closely, it's actually possible to see how they affect each other.

When we have a simple, clear job, we have a very good chance of doing that job well[5,6]. Obviously, we also need to have the knowledge, skills, resources and desire to do it. But, having a simple, clear task initially gives us a massive advantage. There is a plenty of evidence for this, from a wide range of disciplines.

CLARITY IS KEY!

Researchers in management settings have identified that both task clarity[7] and role clarity[8,9] have a significant impact on performance. Have you noticed, when you understand the job, you're able to do it well. When you do the job well, you normally get a sense of satisfaction and fulfilment.

Typically, we human beings like exhibiting mastery and we like to be successful in the things we do. So, when we perform well at something, we tend to want to do it again[10]. Psychologists such as Albert Bandura[11] have identified strong links between mastery, confidence, achievement and motivation.

These links set up a positive spiral, which forms the foundation of our mental game:

- When I am focused on a simple, clear job, I perform really well in that moment.
- When I do this moment after moment, I build up evidence that I'm performing well. This gives me confidence.
- When I am confident in doing something, I am motivated to do it again.

These statements may seem perfectly obvious, but their significance is often overlooked. Even some very well-qualified and experienced people miss the importance of these fundamental principles.

For example, they might try to 'fix' motivation, but struggle because they forget the need for confidence. If someone is not confident in their ability to do the job well, they might well shy away from it.

Think about those tasks that you always seem to put off:

- Do they tend to be tasks that you would consider easy and straightforward?
- Are they tasks that you're confident in, or are they the ones you are not sure about?
- Do they tend to be the tasks you are familiar with, or the ones you would describe as being more difficult or tricky?

The positive spiral shows how you can turn around under performance or deteriorating performance. It tells us that focus is often the best starting point. Most people would probably think that a lack of confidence might best be addressed head on. I suspect you've have seen managers or coaches who believe that a pep talk is a good solution to a team's lack of confidence.

Many people believe that giving someone a pep talk or increasing the amount of positive feedback they receive will help to boost their confidence. Equally, many people would probably think that an inspirational speech or a set of attractive incentives would boost motivation. Although it seems logical on one level, in reality, they don't often have that effect. It does work in the movies – you know, those famous speeches; such as the epic Independence Day speech or the "Inches" speech in Any Given Sunday. The problem is, they don't tend to have a lasting effect in real life situations.

To be honest, many of the ways we try to motivate ourselves and others fail to have any lasting impact. I've seen countless examples where managers in corporations use threats in an attempt to create urgency and elicit more effort from people. Equally, many managers are baffled that doubling the incentive doesn't seem to double the work-rate of their people. I see entrepreneurs constantly seeking new forms of 'inspiration' to recharge their motivational batteries. The very fact they need a regular boost tells us that external inspiration doesn't last either.

Pep talks tend not to be the solution. They rarely have a significant or sustained effect on performance. Research on performance spirals also indicates that verbal encouragement is not often enough to increase confidence or turn around a deteriorating performance[7]. Therefore, it makes sense to start engineering our positive spiral.

The Positive Spiral

Release the handbrake

Motivation

Focus

What pressure?

Love discomfort zone

Confidence

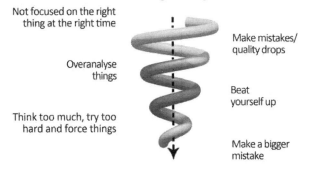

The Negative Spiral

Not focused on the right thing at the right time

Overanalyse things

Think too much, try too hard and force things

Make mistakes/ quality drops

Beat yourself up

Make a bigger mistake

When you're not focused on the right thing at the right time, we often end up making a mistake. When that happens, most people want to know why it went wrong. So, they start to analyse their performance. They beat themselves up. Then they start to over-think their performance, try too hard and force things. As a result, they go and make a bigger mistake. If this keeps going, their performance crashes.

Have you experienced this in your life? Can you remember times when you were not focused on the right thing at the right time? Perhaps you became distracted or you were trying to juggle too many priorities. Did you notice a drop in your performance? Did the quality drop? Did you start making mistakes? If so, how did you respond? Did you beat yourself up, or start to doubt yourself too?

Can you see a reflection of these spirals in your own life?

Of course, if you want to engineer your mindset, you need to understand how all of this relates to your own life experience.

So, how do you start engineering a great mental game. Where does it all begin?

I suspect that you'll have noticed the vital element here, which dictates whether people rise through the positive spiral or slide down the negative spiral.

That's right... it's *focus*.

HOW TO HONE FOCUS

I have found that the best starting point is to simplify the job. Cut out the complexity and start with a straightforward task that is entirely under our control[12]. In fact, it's worth emphasising the words "entirely under our control" again. I can't stress the importance of this enough!

In a team environment, this means that everyone needs to have a simple job. They have to know what they need to do and how to do it.

Do you remember Chris Cook, the swimmer I mentioned earlier? To give you a little background, Chris and I worked together for around seven years.

We met in 2001. He'd just returned from the World Student Games and had come home disappointed with his performance. He had become really anxious before the competitions; he didn't sleep, couldn't eat and was so nervous he would be sick. At that time, he wasn't a star swimmer by any means. He was an average regional level athlete and wasn't on Team GB's radar.

Chris retired from competitive swimming in 2008: his is last competitive race was an Olympic Final in Beijing. As he hung up his swimming cap and goggles, Chris was a double Olympian, an Olympic finalist, double Commonwealth Champion, double Commonwealth record holder and seventh fastest in history in his event.

So, what happened between 2001 and 2008?

Importantly there was one moment early in 2004, which Chris describes as a 'career defining moment'. It was the moment when we actually understood Chris' job. At that point we realised that Chris' job was simply to swim two lengths of the pool as fast as he could... and that was it... nothing else!

Until that moment, we'd been confused.

We thought that his job was to win.

It wasn't!

We thought his job was to make the British team.

It wasn't!

Or, to secure sponsorship or funding.

It wasn't that either!

Chris was a 100m swimmer in a 50m pool. His job was simply to swim two lengths of the pool as fast as he could.

When he just focused on doing that, he became brilliant. That simple task became his single point of focus, every day, for the next four years.

Everything he did, in every training session, every day, contributed to swimming two lengths of the pool as fast as possible.

His job, in *every* competition, no matter how big or small, was simply to swim two lengths of the pool as fast as he could.

And that was it!

Importantly, I also asked Chris to tell me the five key things he needed to do in order to swim two lengths as fast as possible. These were the five most important things; the five that had the greatest impact on his performance.

Once we'd identified his top five, we focused all our energies on improving these.

On competition day, he would simply focus on executing these five key processes as well as he could.

Chris' 'Five Keys' were:

- Start fast
- Fast, but efficient, first length
- Quick turn
- Hold my speed for as long as I can on the second length
- Touch the wall with two hands[1]

---

[1] if he didn't do that in breaststroke he was disqualified

WHAT ARE YOUR TWO LENGTHS OF THE POOL?

What's your job in the simplest possible terms?

Remember, this is not a goal or a target! It is a process, not an outcome. Therefore, it is completely under your control. It is also a complete statement of success.

Once you know your two lengths of the pool, see if you can identify your five keys.

Which are the five most important processes in your performance? Which five have the greatest impact on your performance? If you could only pick five, which ones would you choose?

Once you know these, you have a really powerful way of honing your focus and helping others do the same.

Rather than worrying about winning and losing, what would happen if you simply focused on scoring as many goals as possible and conceding as few as possible?

Instead of hitting a sales target, what would happen if you simply tried to sell as much as you can? What would happen if you focused completely on speaking to as many of the right people as possible, understanding the customer, creating real value for the customer, ensuring the deal was a win-win for everyone and then closing the deal?

Instead of trying to engineer the outcome, what would happen if you focused on executing the processes as well as you possibly could?

If you did that... how good could you become?

So... If you want to hone your focus, start by...

- Simplifying and clarifying your job
- Identifying the key processes
- Focus on executing these as well as you possibly can

HOW TO CONTROL CONFIDENCE

I don't talk about boosting confidence. I talk about controlling confidence. Is your confidence under your control?

Crucially, confidence is built on evidence; not pep talks or affirmation cards. In the 'performance spiral', when you focus on the right thing at the right time, you begin performing well. This gives you evidence that you can do it. It's that *evidence* that fuels your confidence.

So, knowing that confidence is built on evidence, there are a couple of critical questions.

- What evidence are you using to underpin your confidence?
- How can you build a strong bank of evidence, which can power your confidence?

Let's take question one first.

What evidence are you using to underpin your confidence?

Here is a selection of possible sources that you could use. Some of these are under your control. Some are not! Which ones do you have control over, and which are outside of your control?

- Other people's opinions?
- How you compare to others?
- Praise?
- Criticism?
- Your own honest, objective evaluation of your performance?
- Comments on social media?
- Whether you get chosen or selected?
- The score?
- Winning... losing... results?
- Feedback?
- Stats or KPIs?

I would argue that only one of these is genuinely under our control. Can you identify which one it is?

That's right – *your own honest, objective evaluation of your performance.*

The others lie outside of our control. For example, you can't control other people's opinions (although what you do might influence that). Equally, you don't control the result. In sport, the opposition and referee tend to have a significant impact on the score. In golf, the wind might blow your ball off course and land it in a bunker. Arguably, the buyer controls whether you make a sale or not. You don't control other people's feedback (whether it comes in person or via social media). Other people always decide what they say.

If you draw your confidence from these sources, you hand over the remote control for your confidence to someone else or something else. Therefore, your confidence is not under your control.

To bring confidence back under your control, you need to honestly and objectively evaluate your performance. That means detaching yourself from the emotion, either the exhilaration or disappointment, and seeing it for what it really is. This is very different from judging yourself on your results, or on other people's feedback.

If you honestly and objectively evaluate your performance, you can start to answer question two as well.

Let's have a recap of question two.

How can you build a strong bank of evidence, that can power your confidence?

When you evaluate your performance honestly and objectively, you identify those things you did well and those things you want to improve. You could start by giving your performance a score between zero and ten. Zero means "there is nothing good about it whatsoever". Ten means "it's perfect... flawless... can't be improved".

Let's say you scored your performance six out of ten. There will be things you did well, which made your score six and not zero. However, it can't have been perfect because it wasn't a ten. So, there are things you will want to improve. If you identify things you're going to work on, and commit to improving them, you'll come back better. This is a very simple, but incredibly powerful, way of growing your confidence.

To be honest, it doesn't matter whether you score a two or an eight, as long as you don't start to judge yourself. If you score a two, simply identify what you did well and what you're going to work on. Then work on it and know that next time, you'll be better than a two. Then go again. Each time you'll keep getting better.

When you adopt this approach, your confidence comes from the evidence that you are improving.

When I work with elite level athletes (including the world champions and professional players), their confidence often comes from the quality of their preparation. I'll often ask them how confident they are feeling before an event. They normally answer by telling me how well they've practiced, trained and prepared. If they have been highly focused, practiced with real quality, pushed themselves in training and seen improvement, they will feel confident.

If they ducked out of some training or if they know they haven't given their all, they are far less likely to feel confident.

So, if we want to bring confidence back into our control:

- Evaluate your performance, honestly and objectively
- Work on the areas you want to improve
- Know that you've done everything possible in your practice, training and preparation

HOW TO MASTER MOTIVATION

Motivation is often known as 'the why of behaviour'. Therefore, understanding your *'why'* is critical!

Why are you there? Why do you do what you do? Why is it important? Why does it matter? What's your reason?

Your 'why' is critically important because it guides your focus.

Very simply...

Focus follows interest... and... interest follows what you really care about.

If you want to perform well, you need to focus on the process. When you focus on the process, you tend to execute well, and performance follows.

However, it's really tough to focus on the process if you care too much about the outcome. If you focus on the outcome, you are not focused on the process. As a result, you tend to overthink, try too hard, force things and make mistakes.

I once had a conversation with an elite tennis player. He was really struggling with his game. During our conversation I asked him why he played tennis. He told me it was all about winning. In professional tennis, winning is important. Winning equals prize money. If he doesn't win, he won't get paid. However, when we delved a little deeper, he talked about the social importance of winning. He talked about what everyone would think of him if he wasn't winning. He described winning, and his ranking, like some kind of social currency. It gave him a feeling of status and respect from his community. These were the real reasons he played tennis and needed to win.

Then, I said something that sounded ridiculous to him. I said,

> *"You need to be more interested and care more about how you hit the ball, than where it lands".*

Immediately, he started to argue that it didn't matter how he hit it, as long as it landed the right side of the white line. However, as we talked about it a little more, he realised that if he was too focused on where it landed, he wasn't focused on how he hit it.

And, the only way to play decent shots is to focus on how you hit the ball. His challenge, of course, is to care more about the process than he does about the result.

Why?

Because focus follows interest... and interest follows what you really care about.

WHAT IS YOUR WHY?

1. Why do you do what you do?
2. Is it for money?
3. Is it to be the best you can be?
4. Is it to feel successful?
5. Is it to gain respect from others?

It's not only pro tennis players that face this challenge. I see it reflected in many walks of life. For example, sales people who are so focused on closing the deal that they forget about understanding what the customer needs or ensuring the customer will gain real value from their products or service. They forget the processes, dive straight for the outcome and miss it.

I often see recruitment consultants struggle because they really don't like what they do. They don't like the process... they just want the outcome. Therefore, they miss the process and inevitably struggle to get the outcome. Many entrepreneurs fall into the same trap. They want the dream, but don't like the hard yards and the day-to-day processes required to get there.

So, as you can see, having a solid 'why' is vital. Without it, you will struggle to focus on the processes.

But, that's not the only reason your why is critical. If your why (*your reason*) starts to disappear, your motivation tends to go with it. For example, if your why revolves around winning and you start losing back-to-back games, your motivation could start to dry up. If your why revolves around money, and you're struggling financially, your motivation will wane. If it's all about feeling respected, and you're getting criticism... your motivation will evaporate.

When we lose our reason to do something, we start to ask, "What's the point?".

What's the point in working my butt off in training if I'm not winning?

What's the point in putting in all the effort and all the hours if no-one notices?

Why am I bothering if I'm not getting the results?

Motivation is an absolutely vital element of mental toughness.

It powers our tenacity: our ability to keep going when every fibre of our being is begging us to stop.

It underpins our resilience: our ability to get up whenever we get knocked down; no matter how many times it takes.

It impacts on our ability to be composed: to focus on the right thing at the right time, which allows us to make great decisions and execute well when it really matters. So, what is your "why"?

THE ROLE OF FOCUS, CONFIDENCE AND MOTIVATION

Let's have a quick recap.

Focus:

- Simplify and clarify your job.
- Understand your "two lengths of the pool".
- Focus on delivering your "two lengths".
- Focus on the processes – the Five Keys!

Confidence:

- Practice and prepare as well as you possibly can.
- Know that you have a great game plan.
- Know you can execute it.
- Evaluate your performance, honestly and objectively.
- Focus on progress and improvement.
- Don't judge yourself on the results!

Motivation:

- Have a solid "why".
- Remember... Focus follows interest and interest follows what you really care about.
- Do you really care about what you do?

HERE IS WHAT IT ALL LOOKS LIKE IN ACTION

This is an example from an equestrian rider that I worked with a few years ago.

> *"It's two weeks until the competition, which is obviously your big focus at the moment. It's probably fair to say that it is not just a big focus because it's in two weeks' time. This competition also represents your major ambition in the sport at this point, so it has been your focus for years.*
>
> *We discussed how you're feeling about it right now. Your words were 'scared, nervous and worried'. You also talked about the 'pressure of representing this team in such a massive competition'. We spent quite a while chatting about where this all stems from. You talked about missing the opportunity a couple of years ago and not being ready last year. You also talked about the time and money invested into training and competition. You mentioned the pressure that you feel when representing this team; it is high profile ... there are people watching. These are all common reasons why people feel nervous before events. In reality, many people tend to attach a lot of meaning to an event. This acts as baggage and forms an agenda that is not really there."*

As we continued to talk, it became obvious that there were other issues at play as well:

> *"You mentioned that you're not confident in yourself. This is not just true in sport. It has also manifested in*

your life. If we are not confident in life, we tend to pin all of our self-worth on the results we get from sport. In a sense, we look to our sporting success or failure to tell us how good we are at life. In this situation we rely on good results for our self-acceptance and therefore place massive pressure on the performance. As I said, I believe that there is no such thing as pressure. It is created by our imagination. It has to be imaginary because it revolves around the outcome of a future event. Therefore, the only place it can exist is our imagination. And, because we create it, we can also get rid of it! Ultimately, you will feel less pressure to perform in competition when you start to see it for what it really is. The job is actually pretty simple when you look at it – you just need to jump over as many fences as you can, as quickly as you can. If it starts to become more than that, you'll get into problems.

The reality is that the job doesn't change just because it's a major competition. It doesn't change if we put it into an arena with 100 TV cameras and called it an Olympic final, or if it is a training session in your own paddock. We talked about how you can build your confidence and become happy competing. As you said, priority number one is to have fun and enjoy it because that's the whole point in riding!! We also talked about how your performance is dependent upon your focus. If you are thinking 'I hope I don't hit the fence', then you're more likely to hit it. If said to you, 'don't think about the colour blue', then your mind will be filled with blue. The only way to turn this *around is to start focusing on the things that will help you perform. As we chatted about it, you said that you ride at your best when you're focused on the sound of the horses' hooves. If you can really immerse yourself in that sort of focus, your performance will start to take care of itself.*

You also know that you can perform well. You have performed well recently (within the last couple of weeks) and cleared fences that you probably wouldn't have imagined you could clear. Your confidence is built upon evidence. Evidence tells you that you can clear the fences because you do it in training. If you can make training as challenging as competition, you will find it easier to see competition in the same way that you see training. Train like you compete and compete like you train!"

In order to start turning our performance around, you need a very simple starting point. You may see a task as bewildering, maybe even impossible. This is normally a result of getting the job wrong in the first place! (We will explore this in much greater detail later). Simply understanding that our clarity of focus often underpins our confidence is the starting point and understanding that our confidence often underpins our motivation is the next stage.

Here is another example from a session I did with a martial artist, who was frustrated by his recent slump in form:

"In order to help you to break the pattern that you are in, I asked you about the mental baggage that you are carrying at the moment. We started this by talking

about why it is important to win. You said that winning was important because it tells you that you've done what you are capable of. This is important because you know that your training is coming together, and you are heading in the right direction. I asked what the right direction is. You said, 'becoming the British Champion'. I also asked why it's important to become the British Champion. You said that it proves to yourself and everyone else that you can do it. We started to talk about 'everyone else'. You started to tell me about your mates and the blokes at the gym. You also said that until you were 22 you were bullied and that being a martial arts champion would help you to counter that.

The problem is that it creates false pressure. It acts like a sack of bricks on your back, weighing you down. It clutters your mind and creates too much mental noise. It stops you from doing the very, very simple job of fighting the best fight you can. Fighting the best fight you can, on the day, is your ONLY job. The job is not to win. It is not to qualify for anything. It is not to impress anyone or make anyone else happy or proud. Stick to a very simple, clear focus. We chatted briefly about the best point of focus for you. I asked you 'what is the single most important thing you need to focus on when you are fighting?'. You said, 'watch the opponent's eyes'. Keep it simple, watch the opponent's eyes and let your instinct and skills do the rest."

These principles don't just apply to sports. They apply equally to any other walk of life. Here is an example from the first session of an Executive Coaching program with the leader of a high-profile business, who was frustrated because he was working a huge number of hours but struggling to move the business forward at the pace he desired:

"You mentioned that although you know you should focus your attention, you are easily distracted."

I asked this question.

> *"If you had a magic wand, how would things look?'. You started by saying that there really aren't enough hours in the day. You need to start focusing on your workload and being effective with your time. As we discussed this, you mentioned in passing that you are a 'bit of a control freak'. In the same breath, you also said that all of your directors are better than you in their respective fields. You trust them and are happy to let them run with projects. However, you also get yourself sucked into meetings that you don't need to be in.*

> *In our ideal picture we see you with more strategic thinking time and strategic execution time.*

> *You are less involved in proof-reading, answering questions that aren't yours, less tied up in the minutiae and meetings that don't involve you. We also discussed a future where you work closely with your directors to drive corporate objectives. You mentioned spending more time on your visible external*

profile, winning new clients and exploring market op-portunities. It would also allow you to take a more strategic look at the internal structure and culture within the business.

Step one is to clarify and simplify your role to ensure that you can be as effective as possible. We need to sharpen your focus so that you know exactly where you should direct your energies to have the maximum possible impact. Once we do that, you stand a very good chance of both reducing the number of hours at your desk and making more of an impact on the busi-ness. It all starts by understanding where you need to be focused. What are the most effective things?"

SOME HANDY RESOURCES

I've put together a few videos and resources during the last few years, to help you understand how to engineer your head-space. You'll find them on my YouTube channel - @worldclasssimon.

To get you started, have a look at the videos called:

- What's on your iPad?
- Performance spirals
- Hone focus
- Control confidence
- Master motivation
- Pressure

KEY POINTS...

- Focus, confidence and motivation are all fundamental to peak performance.
- Focus, confidence and motivation are all inter-dependent. They require each other.
- Focus underpins confidence.
- Confidence underpins motivation.
- To turn around a performance, it makes sense to go back to basics. Simplify, clarify and focus on the process.

Remember... This is a step-wise process; a system that helps you build mental toughness step by step. Like any process, follow the steps of this stage in order, execute them well and you will find that focus, confidence and motivation will follow.

So, knowing all of this...

What are you going to *do*?

STAGE THREE: ACCOUNTABILITY AND RESPONSIBILITY

Accountability.

Responsibility.

Two commonly used words. Two qualities that most people would say are crucial if you want to be successful.

So, why are they so rare?

The truth is, it is very difficult to develop accountability, unless you have a clear focus. A few years ago, I worked with an English Championship football club. They were struggling. In fact, they were heading for relegation. After one game I listened in to the post-match discussions. The manager was annoyed because the team had lost, and everyone had performed below par.

In a heated discussion, the manager turned to the players and said:

> *"Why will nobody take accountability?"*

When I chatted to the manager later, I asked him to explain each player's job. I asked...

> *"What are the five key things that each player is expected to do.... processes, not outcomes?"*

Unfortunately, the manager and his coaching staff were vague. They did not know exactly what they expected from each of the players. Consequently, they had not told the players what was expected with any clarity. If we have a simple, clear task, we can be held accountable for delivering it. It needs to be clearly defined and it needs to be a process. We need to know what to deliver. Once we agreed the simple, clear processes with each player, we could then hold them accountable for delivering them.

It's vital that we identify processes, not outcomes. I asked the manager what each player was expected to do. By asking this question, I am asking about processes not outcomes. The truth is, you can't hold a team accountable for winning, because it's an outcome. Therefore, it's not entirely under their control. Equally, you can't hold a player accountable for scoring, because that too is an outcome. There are a huge number of elements that are outside of the players' control; such as the quality of the assists they receive and the performance of the opposing goalkeeper.

However, you can hold them accountable for the processes.

WHY IS THIS STAGE SO IMPORTANT?

Those who blame other people and misfortune will not become mentally tough.

Mentally tough people take complete responsibility for their performance. In fact, it goes further than that. In my studies of world-class performers, I discovered that it is a characteristic they all share. Taking responsibility is one of the eight key characteristics that differentiate world class performers. In *How To Shine*[1], Olympic Finalist and Double Commonwealth Gold Medallist, Chris Cook, describes how responsibility and control are inseparable.

Multiple Michelin-star chef, Kenny Atkinson, also explains how he builds mental toughness and world-class standards in his team through accountability and responsibility.

RESPONSIBILITY AND MENTAL TOUGHNESS

How do world class performers develop mental toughness?

Let's take the opportunity to gain a few insights from some of the world's best. We're literally going to lift the lid and understand how they develop mental toughness.

- Kenny Atkinson: multiple Michelin-starred chef
- Chris Cook: double Olympian
- Alan Hinkes: World-leading mountaineer
- Alison Waters: World number three squash player
- Chris Robertson: England Squash's national head coach
- Keir Worth: England Squash's head of performance,
- Bruce Duncan: World-leading adventure racer
- Andy McMenemy: World-record breaking ultra-distance runner
- Ben Saunders: Record-breaking polar explorer

HOW IS MENTAL TOUGHNESS DEVELOPED?

Michelin-starred chef, Kenny Atkinson, explains the process that he uses in the kitchen:

> *"Toughness and resilience comes through maintaining the standards, giving responsibility and making people accountable. I am really pushing the guys here to get the Michelin star. It's not easy. I learned it the same*

way. Chefs pushed me, made me responsible for up-holding standards in my section and held me account-able. You cannot have any excuses, you have to make sure you're on the ball constantly, even though you do not feel up to it some days".

The process that Kenny uses in the kitchen is based on some fundamental principles, such as discipline. Alan Hinkes explains how this also applies to mountaineering:

"I think you can develop toughness, yes. In the mili-tary, it's called discipline, training and drill. Now I think there is a difference between being mentally tough and doing things automatically. To develop toughness, you uphold standards and push people to take on tougher challenges".

These base principles also appear to be central in developing the next group of world-class squash players. Chris Robertson and Keir Worth, from England Squash explain.

Chris says:

"I think toughness can be trained, absolutely. Being on time is important, keeping diaries is important, ex-hibiting a professional attitude, responsibility, atten-tion to detail, how they prepare and do things when they are here. We're looking to see how prepared they are when they play. We are looking for situations where they are challenged. Today, for example, we have situations where lower ranked players are play-ing higher ranked players. The first thing I'm looking for is whether they approach the game the same way

as they normally would. Are they going to take every-thing they can from the match? When things start go-ing against them, which will probably happen, are they going to pack up and go home or are they going to dig in and decide this is the time and it's my last chance to stay in this match? As coaches, we have these off-the-cuff situations, where we decide who stays and who gets cut. Formalising that takes a lot of doing. We will use a lot of video analysis; go back, make notes, assess behaviour, assess reaction to dif-ferent situations, etc.

That's why the upbringing and how they are at home and with their parents has such an impact, because it conditions how you are to be. For me, as a sports coach, you're looking to develop those behaviours all the time. And we can start to build that picture up. We spend time talking to players at those critical mo-ments.

Today players will be put in situations where they have to stand up if they want to be a top player. They will be in tough situations and they will have to re-spond. And if they fail, that's okay, but they learn how to be more tough and that there are parts of the game you have to be tough. They can start to recognise that this is the time I need to give my best and not shirk away. Because if you want to be a great player, you have to answer that challenge".

Keir says:

"Traditionally, we have hoped that it will emerge through the competitive framework. The challenge of tough competition helps to develop a tough mentality. Now though, I think we have to do more than that. I think it emerges with good coaches and what good coaches do on a daily basis with players. Coaches create boundaries, they talk to players about what it acceptable and what is not, behaviour on court and off court, developing players as professionals. It develops through the coach player relationship, which requires a significant amount of coach development. It is crucially important. You cannot get away from the role parents play and their boundaries as to what is acceptable. We do use senior players to help share their experiences to those lower down".

Interestingly, there are common themes that run though all of these accounts; discipline, professionalism, accountability and continual challenge.

Mental toughness is underpinned by traits such as discipline, accountability and professionalism. They are central to success and go hand in hand with responsibility. Viktor Frankl[14] points out that the word responsible ('response-able') means that we are 'able to respond'.

Ultimately, these world class performers know that the responsibility for their success, and in some cases their survival, stops with them.

World number three squash player, Alison Waters:

"Professional squash players are self-employed, so you have to take responsibility for your own performance. When I was younger I used to rely on other people more. I used to spend a lot of time with my coach. I'd turn up for a session and he'd tell me what the session was. That was kinda fine at the time because I was younger and probably needed that help. I guess I did not think too much, I just turned up and trained. Now-a-days I will do my own thing much more. I still have people around me, like my strength and conditioning coach, my physiotherapist and the technical coaches. But I think you get to the stage where there is only so much you can get from others. It's down to me at the end of the day. If I turn up for a coaching lesson now, I will suggest to the coach that we work on this or that. It's changed around now. The coaches won't dictate what we work on, they will ask. It means that I do not turn up for a session for the sake of it, I really need to get something from it.

The physiotherapist could give me endless amounts of programs, but if I do not do them, I will not benefit".

Alison knows that taking responsibility has a tangible importance. Her success on court has a direct impact on her livelihood.

Mountaineer, Alan Hinkes, understands that those who fail to take responsibility may pay the ultimate price.

"With the very best mountaineers and guides, taking responsibility just comes as second nature. I've always accepted that I am responsible for what I do. A lot of

people might think, 'oh well there's a rescue team'. But they cannot always get to you, especially on the big mountains. In Britain you could maybe get away with it, but right from the start I've never wanted anyone to have to rescue me. We've always had the mind that we want to get ourselves off the hill. I guess we were more self-sufficient a few years ago. It was more difficult to get a rescue team in them days.

We'd have to get to the nearest farm, or telephone box to get help and by the time you've done that, you may as well have got yourself off the hill. These days I think people are probably less self-sufficient because they can always get on the cell phone. In the Himalaya there are not any rescue teams, so you have to be self-sufficient. There are not any helicopters. You can't get a helicopter over 6000 meters realistically. You're on your own on the 8000m peaks and that's why I pushed myself to do them, because you're not artificially on your own, you're really on your own. In the UK, you could say that you'll not use your cell phone, but that's a bit artificial. Go to an 8000'er and it's for real."

HOW DOES ALL OF THIS RELATE TO PERFORMANCE?

Australian sport psychologist, Phil Jauncey[15], considers that responsibility and accountability are central to performance. He has worked with many of Australia's leading sports teams, notably in cricket and rugby league. In his book, *Managing Yourself & Others*, Phil argues that many people suffer from a modern day cultural disease; they believe that it's okay to fail, as long as they feel good about it. Rather than looking for ways to address the issues that are causing them to fail, they look instead for excuses. To sum up his point, he says, 'I believe very strongly that everything I do is my responsibility and, therefore, if I do not like what I am doing I can change it'. So, as he suggests, responsibility goes hand-in-hand with control and choice.

Record breaking ultra-distance athlete, Andy McMenemy, agrees:

> *"No-one else can do this. It's me. I've got to get through this. I chose to do this. No-one is making me. It is part of the territory. This is what it takes. If it was easy, everyone would be doing it. I heard a saying that you 'grow through' tough times, not 'go through' them. If I can get passed this, I can do anything. If it was easy, everyone would be doing it".*

These sentiments are shared by polar explorer, Ben Saunders:

> *"In 2003, I did a shorter solo expedition. A solo trip seemed like the ultimate level of challenge. If I was on my own I could not rely on anyone else. It was a two-week expedition. Everything went right. I had more control because it was down to me".*

Double Olympian, Chris Cook was even more direct in his assessment:

> *"We need to cut out that word 'blame'. It really should not come in".*

The message is clear! World-class performers do not blame or make excuses. They take full responsibility for their performance. They also know that responsibility, accountability, professionalism and discipline are absolutely fundamental in developing mental toughness!

SOME TAKE-AWAY MESSAGES...

Multiple Michelin-star chef, Kenny Atkinson

> *"You cannot enforce a standard if you don't know what the standard is".*

> *"We learn from mistakes when we take responsibility for them and accept them".*

> *"Take criticism on board and use it to make you stronger".*

> *"Don't allow yourself to get comfortable".*

Gold medal winning swimmer, Chris Cook

> *"When you take responsibility, something magical happens... you start to take control".*

> *"Champions have a certain work ethic – they are the first ones at training, helping to set up for the session".*

> *"You have to learn from the tough challenges. Sometimes the toughest challenges give the greatest lessons".*

> *"You only learn when you take responsibility for the performance".*

> *"Ego can get in the way if you let it".*

"Failures are actually just a bunch of opportunities".

"Take responsibility for every session, so that you get the most from every moment".

THE TRAPDOOR

It's easy to make excuses or blame something external. Of course, this is particularly common when we're focused on the outcome.

Why didn't you win?

Because the referee made a bad decision.

Why didn't you hit the target?

It was bad luck.

Why didn't you get the sale?

It's not my fault. The customer couldn't afford it.

The outcome, of course, is not in our complete control. So, there could be some very valid reasons why we didn't achieve the outcome. If we start to focus on these reasons and justify why we haven't achieved the outcome, we find ourselves tied up in excuses. In doing so, we become disempowered! In fact, we disempower ourselves!!

How can you take control if you don't take responsibility?

If it's someone else's fault... or something else's fault... you can't do anything about it.

Therefore, to take control, you have to take responsibility. This starts when you ask:

- What did I do?
- What could I have done differently?

You need to evaluate your own performance, not the result. And, no matter what the outcome, you need to ask what you can do to improve.

When you do this, you become "response-able" (as Viktor Frankl would describe it).

QUESTIONS

1. How can you learn from these accounts?
2. How can you develop greater accountability and responsibility?
3. How could you change the question you ask?
4. For example, rather than asking "Why didn't they listen?", what would happen if we asked, "What could I have done to communicate better?"

KEY POINTS...

- When we take responsibility, we take control.
- When we evaluate our performance, we can learn from it and improve.
- We can hold ourselves, or anyone else, accountable for an outcome. We need simple, clear, processes.
- We get tied up in excuses when we justify the reason we didn't achieve the outcome.
- Ego gets in the way!

So, knowing all of this...

What are you going to *do* now?

STAGE FOUR: ENTERING THE DISCOMFORT ZONE

YOUR FOUNDATION

Entering your 'discomfort zone' is often tough. Typically, most people will seek comfort, rather than discomfort. They tend to operate within their comfort zone, rather than push themselves into their discomfort zone. Interestingly, world class performers continually push themselves into discomfort.

When I refer to the discomfort zone, I'm not just referring to physical discomfort. Our discomfort zone can extend to many different facets of our life. Some people are uncomfortable when asked to relinquish control. Others become uncomfortable when they receive critical feedback, or when they are challenged to deliver higher standards. To really start extending yourself, you need to become aware of the depth and breadth of your comfort and discomfort zones.

Of course, when you venture outside of your comfort zone and enter the discomfort zone, your chances of failing sky rockets. When you're in your discomfort zone, trying things you haven't done before or things you aren't very good at, you're more likely to make mistakes and fail. Therefore, if you want to step into your discomfort zone, you need some solid foundations. Firstly, you need to be confident in your own abilities. Let's be honest, if you didn't have a great deal of self-confidence or self-belief, why would you seek out opportunities to fail?

You also need motivation. Your discomfort zone is a tough place to be. Doing things you struggle with is more demanding.

It's harder work. You usually experience more emotional knocks too. Therefore, you need a constant stream of motivation to keep you going. There has to be a very good reason why you're going to keep pushing yourself. As you've also discovered, people who are happy to step outside of their comfort zone are those who are willing to take responsibility for their performance and learn from their mistakes.

If these foundation blocks are missing, it will be tough for people to take significant strides outside of their comfort zone and explore their discomfort zone.

WHY IS THIS STAGE SO IMPORTANT?

Mental toughness is developed when people push their own limits. You're not going to develop mental toughness by staying in your comfort zone! If you want to become tougher, you're going to have to step into discomfort. The up-side is that by continually stepping into your discomfort zone, you start to become ever tougher.

As you push our boundaries, you extend the scope of what you can do. By challenging ourselves to do things you are not comfortable with, you become tougher. During this stage, you will see how world-class performers have pushed through their limits and become capable of extraordinary feats. You may look at some of these examples and think, "I could never do that" (or maybe, "I wouldn't want to do that").

Whilst you may not want to do what they do, it's important to note, you can still learn a lot from them. The strategies they use are available to us all!

LEARN FROM EVERYTHING!

How can we take continual steps into our discomfort zone?

Here are some insights from a genuine sporting legend; Michael Jordan:

> *"I've missed more than 9000 shots in my career. I've lost almost 300 games. 26 times, I've been trusted to take the game winning shot and missed. I've failed over and over and over again in my life. And that is why I succeed."*

Michael Jordan is not alone. Most of the great people who have ever lived, have failed. Many of the greatest entrepreneurs went bust numerous times before they made serious money. The great artists and composers have torn up more work than they ever published. Great athletes always miss more than they score and make more duff shots than perfect shots. And, as Michael Jordan says, that is the reason they succeed[16]!

It is funny how most people hate making mistakes. As human beings, we tend to view mistakes as negative. We tend to view losing as a bad experience. In reality though, it's not the case. I agree that it's usually uncomfortable at the time. It's natural to feel disappointed. Most of us would prefer it if everything worked perfectly all the time. We want things to '*just work*' first time and often get frustrated if the results don't show quickly enough.

Everyone knows that making mistakes is an important part of the learning process. However, there are relatively few people that embrace mistakes and celebrate them, or even who see them as a positive. Common advice is to forget about bad performances and put them behind you. However, the impact of losing or performing badly does often drive people to work harder on their game. And, rather interestingly, research shows that most people learn the least about their performance from victories or successes[17].

One of the characteristics of a truly great athlete is that they learn from everything – the good, the bad and the average. They learn from wonderful performances and dire performances equally. The truly great athletes I've encountered realise that to stay ahead they don't just need to move forwards. They need to move forwards quicker than everyone else, or they'll get overtaken. At the very pinnacle of every sport you'll find athletes who constantly improve their game. They drive themselves to get better after every single training session and every single match they play. If they don't, they know that someone will overtake them.

HOW QUICKLY ARE YOU MOVING FORWARDS?

Are you better than you were at this point

1. Last year?
2. Last month?
3. Last week?
4. Yesterday?

It is probably quite easy to say that you're better than a year ago. But what about a week ago? Have you improved in the last week? Have you used each moment and every opportunity to improve?

There are countless learning opportunities available. They are available to everyone. Some people recognise them and get the benefit of them. Other people miss them.

REFLECTION IS THE KEY!

I often take time out when I'm driving to reflect on the session I've just delivered. I'll switch the music off and silence my phone for a while. It doesn't have to be a heavy exercise. It can be as simple as asking yourself, "what did I do well?", "what do I need to work on?", "how might I do it differently next time?"[16]

In reality, many people don't tend to review their performances on a regular basis or in any real depth. They don't really step back and look at how they are progressing. For professional athletes, the off-season usually provides a good opportunity for reviewing, reflecting and learning the lessons from the competitive season. Lots of people in business do the same at the end of a year or after each quarter. However, relatively few will review each day, or after every meeting, or after each pitch.

Some will do a superficial review. Some will work hard to tease out the real gems. The real value tends to come when we spend a little more time and effort. Daft as it sounds, most people stop before they uncover the really powerful insights.

Why?

To be honest, reviewing our performance can be uncomfortable; especially if you're honest! You may not like some of the things you see. However, when you do review honestly your performance, you start to find opportunities to improve. Once you have done that, your 'personal development plan' starts to write itself. Even better, you know that the time you are spending developing yourself will be incredibly well invested.

It might surprise you to know that a lot of very high-profile (and highly paid) professional athletes do training sessions, or play matches, without really knowing what they are trying to achieve. As a result, they are missing the opportunity to squeeze every ounce of benefit from that session, and missing opportunities to improve. The truly world-class athletes know exactly how each session will help them become better.

HOW TO KEEP IT FOCUSED

Athletes tend to find that there is a close link between the power of their review and their long-term focus. It is very difficult to have clear long-term focus if they are not really sure what they are working on. It is tough to keep focused on training for a long period if they are not sure how each session and each match is helping to make them a better athlete. There are huge parallels in business too. Lots of business people and entrepreneurs don't really have a clear view on how their activities today contribute to the long-term plan, or how they can improve what they do from one day to the next.

You will probably also see how this all impacts on confidence:

- Imagine the difference in an athlete's confidence going into a tough tournament if they know their training has been incredibly focused.
- Imagine how much more confident they will feel if they know that you have been getting better and better week-on-week.
- Imagine how they feel if their previously shaky technique was now rock solid because they've been working on it and testing it for months.

Learning can be uncomfortable for us because inevitably it means making mistakes19. If you only attempt things which you are comfortable with, you will never progress20. Learning does not happen in the comfort zone, it happens in the discomfort zone. You have to push our boundaries. As human beings, we are fantastic learners. We are wired up for learning. Often, we shut down our innate abilities to learn because we get scared to make mistakes or scared to fail.

If you want to become an awesome learner again, go back to basics. Remember how you learned to walk. You stood up and fell over. You fell over a lot! As a baby you kept getting up and falling over. Each time, you would refine it very slightly and then try again. You never gave up. You had no fear of mistakes. Making mistakes didn't make you 'a failure'. So, you kept going and eventually succeeded. If you apply this to your performance and your life, you might be surprised at what you can achieve.

PUSHING THE ENVELOPE AND LOVING YOUR DISCOMFORT ZONE

In stage three, you used some insights from world-class performers, to help us understand how to develop mental toughness. Let's take another glimpse into the worlds of those high achievers you met earlier.

When you push your limits, you virgin territory. You take on challenges you've not encountered before. Your own life experience will tell us that there can be a multitude of demands that you've not experienced and questions that you've never answered. As you push yourself, and leave your familiar territory, the difficulties can become uncomfortable and demand more of us. Polar explorer, Ben Saunders knows that world-record breaking attempts inevitably require him, and his team, to take on an array of challenges that they have never encountered:

> "I really push the limits when I set the bar. It starts in the planning. In 2004 at the age of 26, I set out to cross the Arctic Ocean, from Russia to Canada. At the time there were panels of experts saying that it couldn't be done. Fortunately, no-one told me. Next year we're planning to do a four month, 1,800-mile expedition from the coast of Antarctica to the South Pole and back on foot. It's the first time anyone will have completed it unsupported. When you set the bar that high, everything else scales up; the training, the funding, the number of complications. Therefore, you push the boundaries with everything. We're starting to prepare for the South Pole now. As a team we are going to the Isle of Skye, into the wilderness. We need to build the relationships because the human dynamic will be tested more than ever. When we get to Antarctica,

once we get started, giving up will not be an option. It's
a £1.4 million expedition. We have one shot".

BE PREPARED TO FAIL!

Inevitably, when you push your boundaries you will experience failure. Back in 2012, Kenny Atkinson had been awarded two Michelin stars and was working on a third. Many people would imagine that he was past the point where he failed or made mistakes. However, the reality is significantly different.

Kenny Atkinson:

> *"For new dishes it can take ten or more attempts. Some-*
> *times we will end up just scrapping it. Other times we*
> *might get it right first time, but it's quite rare".*

There is a popular misconception that world-class performers make few mistakes and that they tend to get things right first time. Olympic swimmer, Chris Cook, spent years trying to perfect elements of his race. Here is an excerpt from a presentation that Chris and I delivered:

Simon:

> *"I remember your first GB (Great Britain) cap in Dublin,*
> *when you came eighth in the European Championships.*
> *You were really disappointed with the performance and*
> *especially with your start. I can remember sitting with*
> *yourself and Jock (the coach) in that tiny office behind*
> *the pool, watching the video of the race. We watched*
> *your start, which was pretty terrible. You lost several*
> *meters on the other competitors. But that was the*
> *spark that drove us for years to work on your start. Over*

the course of the next six years, we took a few tenths of a second out of that start. For me, that still has an impact. Most people would say that working for years to take a few tenths of a second off of a start is a long time. We brought in the physiologists, the bio-mechanist and performance analyst, just to take a few tenths off of the start. And then you're going to do the same on your first length, and then on your turn, and then on your return length and the finish. They are the tiny details that take hours to get right, hours and hours. All of that started because you got to the European Championships and failed."

Chris:

Yes, every time I was confronted by a failure, or I didn't quite hit that target, I just viewed it as a bunch of opportunities. It was a chance to take another step forwards. It wasn't quite good enough, but I could find out how to get it good enough".

FAILING IS NOT FAILURE!

A lot of people struggle with failing because they think that failing makes them a failure. Failing and failure are not the same thing! Failing is what happens if you try something and it doesn't work. In itself, failing is not a problem. However, it becomes a problem for many people when they start to view themselves as 'a failure'. If we're not careful, this starts to become part of our identity. We would never refer to ourselves as "a failing", but we might refer to ourselves as "a failure".

I don't know many people that want to view themselves as 'a failure'. It's not a nice way to see ourselves. Nor is it accurate!

If every time we failed, we started to compound the belief that we were 'a failure', we might not seek out opportunities to try something new... push our self into the discomfort zone... and risk failing. But failing does not equal failure.

World class performers don't tend to view 'failing' as 'failure'... or view themselves as 'a failure' just because they tried something and it didn't work. Olympian, Chris Cook, describes failures as 'a bunch of opportunities' to improve and develop. In that respect, many of those at the pinnacle of their field understand the value of failures and mistakes. Far from being negative, mistakes are viewed as essential.

Alison Waters understands the value of her mistakes:

> *"I see mistakes as a positive. Just the other day I did a set of eight exercises that I hadn't done before. I think about half of them felt right, but the other half just didn't feel right. The ones that don't feel right help you to know the difference between feeling right and not. Next time you may only make one or two mistakes in the set. The mistakes help you work out what you need to be doing, so you can work on those little things. You have to have the mistakes to make yourself stronger in a way. If you didn't make mistakes, you wouldn't really learn would you?*
>
> *If you're making mistakes in your training, you must be outside your comfort zone, which is good. That tells me I am pushing hard enough. If I am not making mistakes, I'm probably not pushing hard enough".*

Alison identifies another very important facet. Mistakes help her to know when she's operating outside of her comfort zone. If she's not making mistakes, she's probably not pushing the boundaries. If she's not pushing the boundaries, she's not improving.

World record breaking polar explorer, Ben Saunders, shares that mentality:

> *"If I know how I'm going to do it, the challenge is not hard enough".*

World-class people appear to share a common view of mistakes and imperfections. They do not try to forget about them. They are not aiming to get over them. In fact, their approach seems to be the polar opposite. World-class performers look for them and actively use their mistakes!

OUCH... THAT HURTS!

Often our greatest challenges, and sometimes our greatest falls, provide us with the most powerful lessons. Undoubtedly, these can hurt. Failures and set-backs are not nice experiences often, but they can be incredibly valuable if we make the most of them.

Bruce Duncan also knows that set-backs can hurt:

> *"I guess now; I try to learn from mistakes very quickly. I think it's important to get back on the horse and carry on. Sometimes set-backs hurt. They can be painful. I know that, so I prepare myself for that. I know that I will be in some pain and discomfort, but it will be worthwhile".*

STOP!

Let's go back and read that again.

Bruce says,

> *"I will be in some pain and discomfort, but it will be worthwhile".*

It will be worthwhile! That's why he'll keep pushing himself beyond his comfort zone time after time. He knows the value. He understands why it is beneficial and why it's worth the pain. This gives him the motivation to keep pushing.

It's this perspective that allowed Ben Saunders to get up and dust himself off after his first, rather catastrophic, polar expedition.

> *"We did it on a shoe string. To be honest, it was a complete failure. We didn't get to the pole. I got frost bite. We suffered from hunger. We were attacked by a polar bear. Looking back, we took a bit of a radical approach. It was the first attempt. I was looking at it as an athletic challenge, but I hadn't trained enough, I wasn't prepared, I was inexperienced. There wasn't one big thing that went wrong that caused us to fail, but lots of little things. Looking back, I was young, 23 years old, my metabolic rate was high so I needed many more calories. My equipment and clothing weren't quite right. Lots of little errors, but I could see how it needed to be improved. There is no textbook in polar exploration.*
>
> *The experience left me feeling gutted. I felt like it had been a huge failure. I was physically knackered. Financially it had left me with next to nothing. I was convinced that we'd come home as hero's but there was no 'fanfare'. In hindsight though, I'm glad I had the experience".*

A lot of people in Ben's position may have concluded that polar exploration was not for them. However, Ben simply used the lessons to ensure that he was successful next time. As I write this, Ben is on his way home from Antarctica. He has just attempted, and failed, in a world-record attempt. I'm pretty sure it'll be another step on his journey to success.

WHERE IS THE LIMIT?

As you can see, the challenges that truly extend us, are the also the ones that help us humans grow. Sometimes these challenges are set for us or imposed by circumstance. Sometimes you take them on when they arrive. Other times you might shy away from them. World-class people seem to not only take on challenges when they are presented; they actually seek them out. Ultimately, they realise that their limits are dictated by their perception. They know that 'impossible' is simply a word that's used to describe something they haven't yet done.

World-record breaking ultra- runner, Andy McMenemy explains how he pushed his own boundaries:

> *"The limit is always self-imposed. When I first ran a five-kilometer race, I wondered if I could run a 10k. Then I wondered if I could run a marathon. Some people start to ask if they could run a quicker marathon. I started to ask if I could run further; maybe back-to-back marathons or ultra-marathons? When I did the Marathon de Sables, it was the furthest I'd ever run in a week (151 miles). During Challenge 66, I did my first ever 1000-mile month.*
>
> *You're crossing uncharted territory all the time. When I did three ultras on the trot I was into new territory. The*

first week of Challenge 66 was over 200 miles, so new territory.

Then I was hitting the new milestones with almost every stride. Then doing it all with injuries. All of these experiences pushed me into new territory.

The whole event was like that; the logistics and everything. There were so many times when we thought, 'how the hell are we going to do this?'"

RELISH THE UNKNOWN

Mentally tough people take uncertainty, set-backs and challenges in their stride. They seem to have a different perspective on these experiences. So, how do world-class performers view uncertainty? Here are some of the observations I've made over the years.

- **Uncertainty is normal:** To world-class people, uncertainty is normal. Unlike the majority of us, the very best in the world deliberately seek out uncertainty. They push themselves way beyond their comfort zone. They are always seeking to explore new territory, try new things and go beyond that which has been done before. As such, they are continually surrounded by uncertainty and have normalised themselves to it.

- **Uncertainty provides opportunities:** Creativity actually requires uncertainty. It requires us to move away from what we know. To be creative, and to innovate, we need to break the mould and abandon our familiar territory. Scientists often do this when they disprove theories. They discard what they know (and often what they have built their reputations on) and enter a state of limbo; a state of 'not knowing'.

- **Uncertainty breeds creativity:** Leading organisations realise that the state of uncertainty is a key part of the creative process. They know that when they innovate to create a competitive advantage, that advantage is only temporary. It is lost almost immediately. Almost as soon as they have changed (and created some certainty), they have to change again. In doing so, they dive back into uncertainty.

- **Uncertainty is exciting:** Uncertainty is the reason why people watch sports. If we know the outcome, the spectacle loses its magic. Uncertainty presents us with challenges. It stretches us. Ultimately, of course, it helps us to become better at what we do. The experience of taking on challenges actually drives world-class people and motivates them. They enjoy it!

So, what is it that allows world-class people to continually and deliberately dive into uncertainty?

One answer is; courage. Psychologist, Rollo May[21], understands that uncertainty is often accompanied by anxiety. In psychology, 'hardiness' is said to provide us with the courage to pursue the future, despite its uncertainty.

So, what gives rise to this courage? World-class people will take a leap of faith; a leap into the unknown. They have the courage to jump, not knowing where they will land. They are happy to land wherever they land.

HOW CAN THEY DO THIS?

World-class people continually push themselves beyond their own limits. Their experiences tell them that when they do push themselves beyond the limit of what they previously thought was possible they come out on the other side. By constantly pushing, they have built layer-on-layer of evidence that gives them the confidence to push again.

When you take on any major challenge, you're making an attempt. You don't know whether you will succeed. I suspect it's why we use the term "world record attempts". To world-class people, taking on the challenge is the point. The attempt is the prize. The outcome is less important.

If you took on a challenge and didn't succeed... have you failed?

If you never attempted the challenge... what have you gained?

"Courage is not the absence of fear, but rather the judgement that something else is more important than fear."

In reality, the future is always uncertain, no matter how much certainty we think it may have. In that case, you simply have to choose how you perceive it and respond to it.

HOW DO YOU APPROACH UNCERTAINTY?

Do you adopt the 'bring it on' mind-set or the 'make it go away' mind-set?

That choice, of course, is yours.

HOW CAN YOU DEVELOP COURAGE?

Courage is the ability to step towards those things you're scared of. Like any element of your character, it can be developed. In fact, in *How to Develop Character*, I described how I undid my fear of spiders by deliberately taking steps towards them, not away from them. It started one day when I found a spider in the bath.

Rather than yelling hysterically for help, which I'd done before, I leant on the side of the bath and had a conversation with my eight-legged nemesis.

"This is ridiculous", I said to the spider, "You and me need to come to an understanding". Then, calmly, I called downstairs to my Grandma and asked for some help getting it out of the bath. I wasn't ready to touch it, or even pick it up in a cloth. So, Gran helped me get it out using an upturned class and a piece of card (paper was too flimsy and might bend).

Next time I met a spider in the bath, I remember drawing a big circle around it. Then I got the glass and a piece of card and removed it safely. The time after that, I felt confident enough to draw a smaller circle. Eventually, instead of a glass and piece of card, I challenged myself to pick it up in a cloth... then a piece of tissue paper.

A year of two ago our cleaner screamed down the stairs. "Help, there's a spider in the bathroom". "No problem", I replied. I went up, picked up the spider (no tissue or cloth), and popped it outside.

Over time, I developed courage by continually taking steps towards the thing I was scared of.

If you wanted to develop courage, what challenge would you set yourself?

WHAT CAN YOU LEARN FROM ALL OF THESE EXAMPLES?

The accounts from our world- class people are incredibly revealing. They are not afraid to push their boundaries and work outside of their comfort zone[22]. They know that they are likely to fail. They understand that they will invariably make many attempts before they get it right. Sometimes it will take literally hundreds of hours of work; years of practice. Unlike many people, they embrace the opportunities.

I once asked polar explorer, Ben Saunders, what he felt his biggest lesson had been, to date. The response was telling:

> *"Not being afraid to set big goals. If I know how I'm going to do it, the challenge is not hard enough. Not to be afraid of failure. I have failed far more times than I have succeeded."*

A HEALTHY DISSATISFACTION

The greatest performers are never content. They have a very healthy dissatisfaction with their performance because they know there is always something to work on.

When I ask junior athletes to rate their performance on a scale between zero and ten, many will say 'eight' or 'nine'. When I ask a world champion, they often say 'four'!

Does that mean the junior athlete is better than the world champion, or simply that the world champion has a greater appreciation of the improvements they can still make?

Great individuals and organisations realise that discomfort is temporary. By stepping into their discomfort zone, they eventually become comfortable with whatever it was that caused the discomfort. Essentially, their comfort zone grows to encompass all the things they were not comfortable with. As they begin to feel comfortable, they step into discomfort again.... and so they go on.

HOW DOES THIS ALL WORK ON A DAILY BASIS WITH PEOPLE LIKE ME?

You might be thinking:

"That's okay for all these world class performers, but how does this apply to me and my life?".

Ironically, to answer that question, I'm actually going to use an example of someone who was the best in the world, in his field.

A few years after leaving university, I got a job working with the Newcastle Falcons rugby team. One of our players was a guy called Jonny Wilkinson. At the time, he was the best player in the world. I often watched him practicing; intrigued to see what he did that the other players didn't do (or wouldn't do).

One day, he was practicing kicking the ball into the corner of the field. In rugby, this gives you a real tactical advantage. So, after everyone had finished the training session, Jonny would set up a target with some cones. Then he would challenge himself to land the ball inside the target 20 times out of 20 without missing. He would do this using his right foot and his left foot. Once he hit 20/20, he would make the target smaller and do it again. Again, he challenged himself to hit the target 20 times in a row before he upped the challenge again.

Jonny knows that, in a competitive game, you don't get to pick the ball up and kick it when you're ready. So, he began to make the challenge more realistic. He would ask another player to pass him the ball before he kicked. Interestingly, he asked the player to deliberately make a bad pass (too short, too long, too high, too low) so that he would have to adjust before kicking. Once he nailed 20/20, he asked one of the other players to run at him whilst he kicked to make the challenge even tougher. As always, he kept going until he landed 20/20 in the target.

Then, finally, he would ask the player running at him to start closer. This cut down the time and space he had, which made the kick even tougher.

At each stage, he would step into his discomfort zone. He did this continually, with every element of his training. As soon as he could do something well, he made the challenge tougher.

Remember, these were not giant leaps! These were small, manageable steps. They weren't easy, of course. However, each step was another logical challenge that built on the previous one. On its own, each one was a pretty modest step. But, they all add up. Jonny did this every day. He knows that each little step contributes to becoming the best in the world.

This is a very simple principle.

It can be adopted by anyone.

How does it apply to you and your life?

WHERE IS YOUR DISCOMFORT ZONE?

1. What currently makes you feel uncomfortable?
2. Which things do you tend to avoid rather than approach?
3. When do you tend to feel out of your depth?
4. Does criticism make you uncomfortable?
5. What if you were challenged to be more precise, execute a skill more accurately, consistently or with less time?
6. What if you were challenged to maintain higher standards for a longer period?
7. Are there specific tasks or skills that you find more difficult, or situations that present a tougher challenge?

When you start to answer some of these questions, you begin to appreciate where your comfort zone ends and your discomfort zone begins. It might be that simply answering these questions honestly, and spending time reflecting on them, nudges you into your discomfort zone.

FEELING INVINCIBLE

Something I get asked a lot is:

> *"How do world-class people develop that belief that they can take on 'the impossible'?"*

Good question. Most people quite naturally think that those who achieve extreme success must just be wired differently. Perhaps they just have a different outlook on the world. Maybe they wake up in the morning thinking, "I feel like breaking a world record today – let's go".

That, of course, is the myth.

The truth is that by constantly pushing themselves beyond their comfort zone and towards their limits, they start to nurture a belief. They generate evidence that tells them they can do things they couldn't do before.

Their life experience tells them, "Just because I can't do it yet, it doesn't mean I won't be able to".

They understand that there is a way to achieve those things you can't yet do. There is a simple mechanism. If they use their Discomfort Zone, they can achieve things they've never done before. Then, little steps become bigger steps. As the evidence builds, so does the confidence. After a while, our mindset changes. We start to look at challenges differently. If we've taken on some really tough challenges... ones we never thought we'd be capable of... our perspective changes. Then we look at those 'impossible' challenges differently. Instead of saying, "There's no way I could do that", we start to ask, "Why not? Let's give it a go. What have I got to lose?".

KEY POINTS...

1. Keep challenging yourself to take small, manageable steps into your discomfort zone.
2. When you do this your comfort zone will grow to encompass those things that used to be uncomfortable. Once that happens, step again.
3. When you keep doing this, you develop the confidence that you can keep stepping.

4. Little steps can become bigger steps. As we take on bigger challenges, we develop confidence and belief.
5. After a while we take a completely different view on the word "impossible".

So, knowing all of this...

What are you going to do now?

NOTES

STAGE FIVE: TOUGHNESS – RESILIENCE, TENACITY AND COMPOSURE

A SOLID FOUNDATION

By this point, much of the work has been done. When you understand what mental toughness looks like, sounds like, thinks like and acts like, you can start challenging yourself to become tougher. When you have a solid mental game, you're able to consistently perform at your best. That is an important part of mental toughness! Simply by being focused, confident and motivated consistently, you become mentally stronger.

By becoming accountable and responsible, you are able to take control and ensure that you learn from everything. This helps you to make the most of your experiences and bounce-back from 'set-backs' stronger. As a result, you're also more willing to seek your discomfort zone and start to truly push your limits. These are the characteristics that come together to form mental toughness.

WHY IS THIS STAGE SO IMPORTANT?

During this final stage, we will look at how to display composure, resilience and tenacity when we face the most demanding challenges. In particular, we will look at the concept of 'pressure'. We will identify strategies that can help us to perform at our peak in any situation. In addition, we'll look at how some of the toughest people in the world develop extreme mental toughness. This is the icing on the cake!

MENTAL TOUGHNESS IN ACTION

Right at the start of Master Mental Toughness, I shared the key elements that I see in mentally tough athletes. Those with mental strength will push themselves to their limits and thrive in adverse conditions. Those people also tend to take on the most demanding challenges, rather than back away. They will take responsibility for their performance and use criticism to get better. In demanding situations, those who have mental toughness will tend to be composed. They make better decisions and execute skills to a consistently high standard.

Can you remember the six signs of mental toughness that I see in athletes, which are built into the 'mental toughness matrix'?

1. Athletes who consistently perform at their best in adverse conditions.

Mentally tough athletes tend to be focused, confident and motivated, whatever the situation. Every athlete experiences their peaks and troughs, whether that is through injury, lack of form, de-selection, a run of poor results, or whatever. Every athlete has been in situations where the chips are down and they have their backs to the wall. Mentally tough athletes tend to apply themselves consistently, whether they are on a high, or at the bottom of the deepest low.

2. Athletes who come back stronger from set-backs.

Athletes with mental strength tend to display 'bounce-back ability'. I have come to realize that great athletes seem to experience the same amount of 'good luck' and 'bad luck' as everyone else. However, their response to their 'luck' is normally different. When they experience set-backs, mentally tough athletes knuckle down, apply themselves, learn as much as they possibly can from the experience and grow from it.

3. Athletes who are composed in 'pressurised situations'.

When athletes perceive that they are under pressure, some will panic. Sometimes the game plan flies out of the window and they start to make strange decisions and unforced errors. Mentally tough athletes, however, tend to have the ability to remain composed. They tend not to panic, they stay on task, keep focused and stick to the game plan. When they make mistakes, they simply focus back onto the task in hand and execute their skills.

4. Athletes who actively seek out, and thrive in, their discomfort zone.

Some athletes will respond well if they are pushed outside of their comfort zones. Truly great athletes go a step further. They actively seek out opportunities to push themselves into their discomfort zone. The world class athletes that I've worked with will say that the alarm bells start ringing when they become comfortable. These people relish the challenge and go looking for it!

5. Athletes who push to their limit, not just the point of discomfort

Most people stop when things become uncomfortable. Although we think of this in a physical sense (i.e. the point we become tired or feel physical pain), this concept extends to other limits too. Some people give up when they've tried a new skill a few times and it's not worked perfectly. They don't like the feeling of 'failing' because it is uncomfortable. Other people keep going and keep failing, until they get it right.

They don't stop at the point where it becomes uncomfortable, they stop when they hit their limit.

6. Athletes who are self-critical and seek critical feedback from others

Some athletes are uncomfortable with criticism. Others will listen, take criticism on board and acknowledge it. The better athletes will recognise that it is a gift and use it to its fullest extent. The world class athletes that I've met actually seek out critical feedback and then squeeze every possible ounce of benefit from it. To them, critical feedback is like oxygen. It fuels their development. Without it they know they cannot grow.

When we look at the clues, it's possible to see the three of the critical components of mental toughness;

- Composure
- Resilience
- Tenacity

What do these three words mean?

Composure:	The ability to consistently make optimal decisions and to execute skills to a high standard, whatever the situation.
Resilience:	The ability to bounce-back from set-backs and to thrive in adversity.
Tenacity:	The ability to push to the limit and refuse to quit.

So, how do you develop these three critical elements?

Firstly, you may have noticed that the way you develop accountability, responsibility and the ability to love your discomfort zone uses the same basic method. In fact, it's the way you develop any characteristic.

You develop our character when you take on challenges. Specifically, it is the choices you make when you encounter challenges that really shapes your character.

So, by applying this simple principle, you can develop these three vital characteristics.

COMPOSURE

In order to make optimal decisions and execute skills to a high standard, you need focus! When performance deteriorates, it is often because you're simply not focused on the right thing at the right time. The truth is, you are always focused on something. The question is, are you focused on the most effective thing in each moment?

In stage two, you learned how to hone focus. Focus is fundamental to composure. In a sense, composure is simply the ability to focus in more demanding situations. If you cannot focus effectively, you'll find it really tough to do when the challenge increases.

So, how can you develop the ability to remain composed in critical moments? What challenges can you set yourself?

Here is an example of how I developed composure in a trio of cricketers.

I took them to the golf course. Specifically, we went to the putting green. I gave them a very simple task; to make as many consecutive two-foot putts as possible. There's a very good reason why I chose a two-foot putt. It is not a difficult skill. If you miss a putt from just two-feet, it's not a lack of skill. It's a lack of focus. To demonstrate this, I asked the three players to putt as many as they could without missing. When it was just the two of us, out on the green, with no-one else watching, they would typically nail 75-100 shots in a row.

However, this doesn't really test their composure. To help them develop composure, I need to challenge them to complete this very simple skill 'under pressure'. Of course, pressure doesn't actually exist – we imagine it. So, I created some situations... played around with the psychological environment... which might tempt them to imagine pressure. If this happens, they're likely to lose their focus and miss the putt.

Firstly, I created a sense of competition. There was no trophy or prize money. However, the first one to miss would be "the loser". These were competitive players. None of them wanted to be labelled "the loser". So, even this little competitive edge impacted on their composure. Interestingly, from scores of 75-100, the first player missed on 14.

Then I would work with them for a while to equip them to meet this demand, before increasing the challenge.

Next, we added a little spice to the competition. Each player brought a £20 note and placed it in an envelope. It's not a vast amount of cash, but it is enough to heighten the sense of competition. Even a little tweak like this can tempt them to focus on the outcome rather than process. As a result, the first player missed on six.

And then, of course, I worked with them so that they could meet this level of challenge before upping the ante again.

I knew that each of the players had an 'Achilles heel'. For example, one of them was particularly concerned about what the Director of Cricket and the First Team Coach thought of him. It was the final year of his contract and he wanted to impress. So, I invited them along to watch the challenge. I explained that Martyn (the Director of Cricket) and Jason (the First Team Coach) wanted to know how composed they were because Martyn needed to decide who got contracts and Jason was picking the team. Then I simply said, "Off you go. Putt as many as you can without missing". The player who was in the last year of his contract missed the first shot.

I also knew that one player was particularly bothered about what his team-mates thought of him. He desperately did not want to let the team down. So, I created the 'Don't Let The Team Down Challenge'. Each player had a team. However, our trio were the only ones that could putt the ball. If they missed, the team got the consequence. On this occasion, that meant buying coffees for the other players and carrying all the bags on their upcoming pre-season tour. Of course, the teams standing behind our three players definitely did not want to be buying the coffees for everyone else or carrying their bags. In fact, the teams would stand behind their player muttering, "Don't you miss!". As you might expect, the player who was really concerned what his teammates thought of him missed his first shot.

At each stage, it is important to build your ability to perform in those conditions, before increasing the challenge. This is where you actually develop the composure. Keep challenging yourself to become comfortable in a challenge that was previously uncomfortable.

Finally, we created an 'ultimate' challenge that mirrored the demands of competition. In our stadium, right in front of the main stand, there are water jets that sprays the field. Each jet has a little grass plug. If you take the grass plug out, it reveals a hole that's approximately the size of a golf hole. So, we set up a challenge. Complete as many two-foot putts as you can in front of the crowd. We chose our biggest game of the year. The stadium was packed. The fans had been drinking for a couple of hours and were pretty vocal. I placed a sign behind the players saying, "Boo me if I miss" and we invited the TV cameras over to record the action.

And.... no-one missed.

We only had around ten minutes, during a break in the game. Each player completed around 40 putts and we ran out of time.

It shows how much composure the players had developed through the series of challenges.

HOW CAN YOU USE A SIMILAR APPROACH TO DEVELOP YOUR COMPOSURE?

1. What kind of challenges could you set yourself?
2. How can you gradually increase the level of challenge?
3. Where is your 'Achilles heel' and how can you challenge it?
4. What's your 'ultimate' challenge?

RESILIENCE

Resilient people approach challenges and set-backs by looking for the opportunities. They tend to ask, "how can I?" or "how could I?" rather than "why can't I?"

Here's an example, from my work as a sport psychology coach:

"A few years ago, I worked with a world-class Olympic swimmer, who was ranked in the top ten in the world for his event. He had sustained a back injury that threatened to end his competitive year. His injury meant that he could not swim more than a couple of lengths before succumbing to the pain. Many swimmers would imagine that being unable to swim would be a show-stopper.

I chatted with him about the injury for a while. During my career I have worked with some Paralympic athletes. Whenever I start working with them, I begin by asking them what they can do. Many people might start by asking a disabled athlete what they cannot do, but I've always done the opposite. Therefore, I decided to take the same approach with the injured swimmer.

Through the course of the conversation, we discovered that there were many things that the athlete could still do. In fact, this injury gave him an opportunity to work on a few skills that he rarely had the chance to practice, such as sculling. When sculling, swimmers keep their body and legs rigid, and only move the water using their hands and arms. It is a skill that helps them to move water more effectively and therefore to become quicker.

So, together we reworked his training program to build on the things the athlete could do. Once his injury subsided, he found that he was significantly quicker because he'd used the time to work on his skills".

Resilient athletes find a way to come back stronger! They always find a way to learn something or gain something from each experience. They see the opportunities to become better because they are always looking for them.

How can you learn to become more resilient?

It's worth remembering that resilience is our 'bounce-back-ability' and our ability to perform well in adversity. Life has a habit of throwing us curve-balls. Shit happens! During the natural course of life, there is a pretty good chance that you'll experience adversity and get knocks. Things won't work out as you expect, or as you have planned. You'll get knocked down.

The question is:

- How do we respond when that happens?
- Do we roll with the punches?
- Do we get back up and go again?

As Sir Winston Churchill once said...

"Success consists of going from failure to failure without loss of enthusiasm".

What would it take to blunt your enthusiasm?

If you remember that your character is shaped by the choices you make when you hit challenges, you need to understand how you respond in those moments. It's easy to say the words, "bounce back when you get knocked".

Lots of people know that's what they need to do, but they struggle to do it. If you want to make a change and become more resilient, you need to know how to engineer our head-space in the critical moments.

- What's going through your mind when you get knocked down?
- What thoughts are occupying your mind?
- What's the conversation between your ears?

Are you thinking,

> *"Don't make me get back up. I don't want to. I'm tired. It hurts.... Please someone, just take it away"?*

Or, do you tend to think,

> *"Okay, I'm not going to let this beat me. I can learn from this. It can serve me. What can I learn? How can this experience make me stronger?"*

Take a moment to think about the conversation between your ears during those moments when you've shown the greatest resilience. Think back to a time in your life when you encountered real adversity and rose to the challenge. Or, a time when you got knocked down and bounced back stronger. How were you thinking?

What if we used the strengths that we already possess and build on those? What if you pressed pause next time you faced adversity, and decided to think the way you did when you were at your most resilient?

It's wise not to expect perfection. Remember, learning this is like learning to walk. If at first you don't succeed, tweak it and try it again... then tweak it and try it again. Use life's curve-balls as an opportunity to practice, experiment with a few ideas and refine your approach. If you can do this, you'll start to "grow through adversity, rather than go through adversity", as Andy McMenemy describes it.

To help, here are some tips:

- Stop judging! If you've decided that a situation is 'bad', you'll tend to see the threats and it'll be harder to find the opportunities.
- The opportunities that you'll find tend to relate to processes; for example, a chance to work on your skills. Those who are focused on their processes, tend to see the opportunities.
- If you're only motivated by the outcome (or the result) these opportunities are harder to spot.

TENACITY

Tenacious people will push themselves to the limit and won't quit until they've given it their all.

I remember watching my home-town football team recently in a Cup match. With around five minutes to go, the opposition scored and took a 2-1 lead. All of a sudden, my team kicked into action. The energy levels and urgency picked up. They ran harder. They were more physical. The full backs started to over-lap. Midfielders started getting into the penalty box and players all over the field made 'heroic' tackles to get the ball back.

Do you think that is tenacity?

Personally, I don't think so. I asked myself why they needed to go behind on the scoreboard before they put their foot on the gas. Why weren't they doing that five minutes earlier? Clearly the players had the energy to do it. Physically they were capable. Obviously, they were not pushing themselves to the limit and giving every last ounce of energy for the whole 90 minutes.

Tenacious players would not wait until they needed to give more. Tenacious players give everything they can anyway.

So, what are the secrets to tenacity?

World-leading adventure racer, Bruce Duncan, says:

> *"If you want something enough, nothing is too much hard work, nothing is too painful."*

This highlights a vital point; motivation is key! Crucially, we have to be motivated by the right reason, in order to develop tenacity.

Question: Which of these motives is likely to give us the more tenacious athlete?

- The desire to win

    or

- The desire to achieve their potential Some people might say, "the desire to win".

Others might disagree, with very good reason:

- What happens if the athlete looks dead and buried in the competition?
- What happens if the athlete is cruising to victory?

If an athlete is motivated by a desire to win and they can't see any hope of victory, they're very likely to give up. If they don't believe they can win, they might ask, *"What's the point in giving everything? I'm going lose anyway".*

Equally, if they're winning easily, they are more likely to take their foot of the gas and hit cruise control rather than giving every last drop of effort.

Arguably the stronger driver is the desire to achieve your potential.

THE FOUNDATION

Throughout *Master Mental Toughness*, I have emphasised that each stage of the process provides the foundation for the next stages. Just like building a staircase, each step has to be constructed properly if we want to create a strong structure.

As you know:

- Composure is underpinned by focus and confidence
- Resilience is also underpinned by focus (particularly focus on processes) and a desire to learn from everything (which is underpinned by motivation)
- Tenacity is underpinned by motivation

Remember, focus follows interest and interest follows what you really care about.

All of this pulls us back to that fundamental question again.

What's your 'why'?

MY PERSONAL EXPERIENCE

In the Introduction, I mentioned that I have been challenging myself to develop mental toughness. A few years ago, I became aware that I'd never really pushed myself to my limits. It really dawned on me when I began studying world class performers. I could see that their ability to keep pushing, no matter what, enabled them to be great. When I looked at myself, I realised that I would often give up and back off when things became too uncomfortable. If I wanted to be successful, I knew this is something I needed to work on. So, I decided to challenge myself.

I was always pretty sporty as a kid. I was never a stand-out performer but enjoyed it. In my late teens I played a little semi-professional football and rugby. So, I thought I'd set myself a physical challenge. After meeting world-record breaking ultra-marathon runner, Andy McMenemy, I embarked on a daft 40-day endurance challenge around the UK.

It involved kayaking from London to John O'Groats (at the northernmost tip of Scotland), then cycling from John O'Groats to Land's End (the southern-most tip of England), then running from Land's End back to London. I wrote a book about the whole experience, called '*Could I Do That*?'.

That challenge really helped me to understand what goes on between my ears when I hit those really tough moments.

- What happens when the doubts come flooding in?
- What happens when you 'hit the wall' and you still have five miles left to run?
- What is the conversation between my ears?

How do I change the conversation when I start thinking:

"I've run out of gas... I can't go on"?

Whilst I don't want to spoil that book for you, I will tell you that I didn't end up completing the 40-day challenge. During the training, my wife became seriously ill and I made the decision to put the whole thing on hold. I needed to look after her and my two young girls. The challenge was important to me... but it wasn't more important than my wife's health or looking after my daughters.

To be honest, I found out a lot about myself during that challenge. However, not completing it left me with a feeling of unfinished business. So, a few years later I embarked on a different, but equally nutty, endeavour. This one had a few parameters. Knowing that my wife had not recovered, I needed to be able to do the training in smaller blocks (a few hours at a time, rather than spending the whole day training), so that I could be around to look after her and the girls. And, the event itself had to be done inside a day (rather than needing to be away for 40 days).

So, the challenge I set myself was to walk 100 miles in 24 hours.

After fifteen months of training, the day arrived. At 9pm on a Friday evening in the height of summer, I strapped by pack on my back and started walking. My 100-mile route was composed of a 12 ½ mile lap, which I would do eight times. It started and finished at my house. I deliberately engineered eight tempting opportunities to give up. You see, the whole reason for this challenge was to help me navigate through my 'quit point'. I wanted to encounter that moment when I would be most tempted to give up. I wanted to learn how to navigate through it and out the other side. And, I knew that there were likely to be multiple, and ever-tougher 'quit points' on a 100-mile walk.

I hit the first major 'quit point' at the half-way mark. I'd just changed clothes, refilled my pack and been to the toilet. Less than a mile into the second half of the walk my body seized up. I had shooting pains down the side of each leg. It felt like a spear was being jabbed into my left knee. Every single step was excruciatingly painful. I hobbled along for a few meters hoping it would ease, but it just got worse. Around a mile later, my mind started rebelling…

> "You can't possibly go on like this"

> "Just stop. You might be doing some serious damage to yourself".

> "No-one's watching. You're not going to lose face".

> "You've done really well to get to 50 miles".

> "You're only a mile from home. Just turn back".

Interestingly, I noticed that my mind was coming up with all sorts of arguments to justify quitting. It was almost like my mind was offering me some mental painkillers, to dull the pain I'd feel if I failed.

As the pain built even further, I asked myself what I would say to a client in this position. I am a great believer that we would all be brilliant if we simply took our own advice. So, I began coaching myself. Then it dawned on me.

There are two critical questions that you need to answer when you hit the 'quit point'.

- Why are you doing this?
- How much do you want it?

In Viktor Frankl's words, "Those with a 'why' to live, can bare almost any 'how'". Viktor Frankl spent years as a prisoner in Auschwitz. He saw the true depths of human suffering and those who survived it. Those with a reason to live seemed to find a way.

So, what was my 'why'?

Why was I doing this?

Why was I subjecting myself to this pain?

Then of course I remembered. It was to help me navigate through my 'quit point'. And, here I was. This was the quit point. Then I asked myself:

> *"How much do I want to be able to get through this?*
> *Is this worth the pain?".*

Yes.

Almost as soon as I'd made that decision, my mind began working for me. Instead of finding justifications to give up, it started to solve a different problem. My mind seemed to accept that I was going to keep going, so it began seeking ways to help me continue.

The conversation between my ears changed to:

> *"How can I get rid of this pain?"*

> *"How about stretching?"*

> *"Where's a good spot?"*

> *"I could stretch on that gate!"*

> *"Have I drunk enough water?"*

> *"Would eating a banana help?"*

And, off I went again. Each time I encountered an opportunity to quit, my mind would go through a similar process. However, I noticed that the rebellious thoughts were not as intense the next time, and even less intense the time after that. Towards the end the conversation sounded more like...

"We could just go home... Okay, you're not going to, are you? Let's keep going then".

This understanding now helps me whenever I get close to my 'quit point'. I'm not just talking about physical challenges. It applies equally to challenges in my life and in my business. I've become a more tenacious person. With these new levels of tenacity, I was able to deliver a conference event for 250 business leaders in London earlier this year.

There were loads of points where I thought about pulling the plug on it because I'd start to think...

"It's too risky"

"What if we don't fill the room?"

"What if we don't make break-even?"

"What if this ends up costing us a fortune?"

"Maybe we ought to pull out before we get in too deep".

But, I didn't quit. It was incredibly hard work, but the event was a massive success. That's how I've done it. How does all of this work for you?

BUILD YOUR MENTAL TOUGHNESS JIGSAW

Challenge	How have you responded in the past?	How would you respond now?
You encounter a challenge that you've never come across before.		
You hit rock bottom.		
You fail publicly.		
You are faced with a seemingly impossible challenge.		
You find yourself becoming anxious and feeling 'under pressure'.		

Those are some hypothetical examples. I'd invite you to identify the challenges that you are experiencing at the moment. How can you use what you've learned to help you respond to your current challenges...?

Challenge	How have you responded in the past?	How would you respond now?

A FINAL THOUGHT

Many people struggle to bridge the gap between what they know and what they do.

I'm pretty sure you didn't buy this book so that you could 'know' mentally tough. I'm pretty sure you want to *be* mentally tough. Bridging that gap requires us to practice what we know. If you ever want to draw on a skill, when it really matters, you need to have practiced it so many times that it becomes natural... so that you don't need to think about it. The same is true with all of the components that make up mental toughness. Practice is key!

Okay, the time for talking is over...

It's time to DO it!

As human beings, we learn many things in the same way we learned to walk. Learning to walk requires us to fall over, make mistakes, learn from them and go again.

It's exactly the same with mental toughness.

If at first you don't succeed, change and try again... then change and try again... then change and try again.

Keep going until you succeed!

Remember...

"Giving up is not the result of failure, it is the cause".

BIBLIOGRAPHY

[1] Hartley, S.R. (2012) *How To Shine; Insights Into Unlocking Your Potential From Proven Winners*, London: Capstone.

[2] Sheard, M. (2012) Mental Toughness: *The Mind-set Behind Sporting Achievement (2nd Edition)*, London: Routledge.

[3] Hammermeister, J,. Pickering, M, and Lennox, A. (2011) *Military Applications of Performance Psychology Methods and Techniques: An Overview of Practice and Research*, Journal of Performance Psychology, 3, 3-13

[4] Ankersen, R. (2011) *The Gold Mine Effect; Unlocking The Essence of World Class Performance*, London: Rasmus Ankersen.

[5] Donnelly, J.H. and Ivancevich, J.M. (1975*) 'Role Clarity and the Salesman'*, Journal of Marketing, 39(1), 71-74.

[6] Baumeister, R.F. and Showers, C.J. (1986*) 'A review of paradoxical performance effects: Choking under pressure in sports and mental tests'*, European Journal of Social Psychology, 16(4), 361-383

[7] Lindsley, D.H., Brass, D.J. and Thomas, J.B. (1995) *'Efficacy-Performance Spirals: A Multilevel Perspective'*, Academy of Management Review, 20(3), 645-678.

[8] Bray, S.R. and Brawley, L.R. (2002a) *'Role Efficacy, Role Clarity and Role Performance Effectiveness'*, Small Group Research, 33(2), 233-253

[9] Bray, S.R. and Brawley, L.R. (2002b) *'Efficacy for Independent Role Functions: Evidence from the Sport Domai*n, Small Group Research, 33(6), 644-666

[10] Kloosterman, P. (1988) *'Self Confidence and Motivation in Mathematics'*, Journal of Educational Psychology, 80(3), 345-351

[11] Bandura, A. (1997) *Self-efficacy: The exercise of control*, New York: Worth Publishers.

[12] Horn, T. (2008) *Advances in Sport Psychology, Champaign*, IL: Human Kinetics..

[13] Key, A. (2006) *'Knowing Your Role In Rugby',* Rugby Football Union Technical Journal. 1-6.

[14] Frankl, V. E. (2004). *Man's search for meaning,* London: Rider.

[15] Jauncey, P. (2002) *Managing Yourself & Other*s, Brisbane: CopyRight Publishing.

[16] Hartley, S.R. (2011*) Peak Performance Every Time*, London: Routledge.

[17] Halden-Brown, S. (2003) *Mistakes Worth Making: How to turn sports errors into athletic excellence*, Champaign, IL: Human Kinetics.

[18] Orlick, T. (2000) *In Pursuit of Excellence: How to Win in Sport and Life Through Mental Training* (3rd Edition), Champaign, IL: Human Kinetics.

[19] Colvin, G. (2008) *Talent is Overrated: What Really Separates World Class Performers From Everybody Else*, New York: Portfolio.

[20] Cotterill, S. and Johnson, P. (2008) *'Exploring the Concept of the Comfort Zone in Professional Soccer Players'*, Association for Applied Sport Psychology Annual Conference. St Louis, USA

[21] May, R. (1975) *The Courage to Create*, New York: W.W.Norton.

[22] White, A. A. K. (2009) *From Comfort Zone to Performance Management*, New York: White & MacLean Publishing.

REFERENCES

Ankersen, R. (2011) *The Gold Mine Effect; Unlocking The Essence of World Class Performance*, London: Rasmus Ankersen.

Be World Class Conference (2011) *'Bruce Duncan...on Mental Toughness',* 6th October 2011. Online. Available HTTP: http://www. beworldclass.tv (accessed 31st January 2012).

Beilock, S. (2010) Choke, New York: Free Press.

Boelen, P. A. & Reijntjes, A. (2009) *'Intolerance of uncertainty and social anxiety',* Journal of Anxiety Disorders, 23, 130-135

Bull, S. J. (1996) *The Mental Game Plan: Getting Psyched for Sport, London*: Sport Dynamics.

Christenson, M. (2010) *'World Cup 2010: Capello says pressure hindered England players'*, The Guardian. 21st June 2010.

Colvin, G. (2008) *Talent is Overrated: What Really Separates World Class Performers From Everybody Else*, New York: Portfolio.

Cotterill, S. and Johnson, P. (2008*) 'Exploring the Concept of the Comfort Zone in Professional Soccer Players',* Association for Applied Sport Psychology Annual Conference. St Louis, USA

Csikszentmihalyi, M. (2008) *'Creativity, fulfillment and flow'*, Keynote presentation to TED Conference. 24th October 2008. Online. Available at: http://www.youtube.com/watch?v=fXIeFJCqsPs [Accessed 15th December 2010]

Engh, F., 2015. *The Coach Who Became 'Best Man'*.
Online. Available at: http://www.huffingtonpost.com/fred-
engh/the-coach-whobecame-best_b_8216402.html [Accessed
18th October 2015].

Fisher, M. (1998) *The Golfer and the Millionaire*, New York:
Cassell Illustrated.

Frankl, V. E. (2004). *Man's search for meaning*, London: Rider.

Gerrard, S. (2010*) 'England skipper Steven Gerrard tells under-
fire stars to make their nation proud ahead of do-or-die
showdown with Slovenia'*, Daily Record. 23rd June 2010.
Online.
Available HTTP: <http://www.
dailyrecord.co.uk/football/world-cup-
2010/news/2010/06/23/englandskipper-steven-gerrard-tells-
under-fire-stars-to-make-their-nationproud-ahead-of-do-or-
die-showdown-with-slovenia-86908-22353116/>

[accessed 15th December 2010]

Halden-Brown, S. (2003) *Mistakes Worth Making: How to turn
sports errors into athletic excellence*, Champaign, IL: Human
Kinetics.

Hammermeister, J,. Pickering, M, and Lennox, A. (2011)
*Military Applications of Performance Psychology Methods and
Techniques: An Overview of Practice and Research*, Journal of
Performance Psychology, 3, 3-13

Hartley, S.R. (2010) *'Athletic Focus & Sport Psychology: Key To
Peak Performance'*, Podium Sports Journal, December 2010.
Online. Available at:
http://www.podiumsportsjournal.com/2010/12/09/athleticfo

cus-sport-psychology-key-to-peak-performance/> (accessed 21st December 2010).

Hartley, S.R. (2010) *'Learn From Everything'*, Squash Player, 38(6), 24.

Hartley, S.R. (2011*) Peak Performance Every Time*, London: Routledge.

Hartley, S.R. (2012) *How To Shine; Insights Into Unlocking Your Potential From Proven Winners*, London: Capstone.

Hartley, S.R. (2013) *Could I Do That?,* London: Capstone.

Hartley, S.R. (2015) *How To Develop Character; Beyond Skills, Knowledge and Personality*, Wetherby: Be World Class.

Heath, R. (2009) *Celebrating Failure: The Power of Taking Risks, Making Mistakes and Thinking Big*, New Jersey: Career Press.

Huw, J. (2010) *'Rugby World Cup 2011. Are the All Blacks Peaking Too Soon?'*, Suite101.com, 2nd August 2010. Online. Available at :
http://www.suite101.com/content/rugby-world-cup-2011--are-the-allblacks-peaking-too-soon--a268927> [accessed 15th December 2010]

Jauncey, P. (2002) *Managing Yourself & Others*, Brisbane: CopyRight Publishing.

Johnson, S. R. et al., 2011. *A Coach's Responsibility: 'Learning How to Prepare Athletes for Peak Performance'*, The Sport Journal.

Jones, G., Hanton, S., & Connaughton, D. (2002). *'What is this thing called Mental Toughness? An investigation with elite performers'*, Journal of Applied Sport Psychology, 14, 211-224.

Jones, G., Hanton, S., & Connaughton, D. (2007). *'A framework of Mental Toughness in the world's best performers.'* The Sport Psychologist, 21, 243 – 264.

Jowett, S. & Cockerill, I., 2003. *'Olympic medallists' perspective of the althlete–coach relationship',* Psychology of sport and exercise, 4(4), pp. 313-331.

King, J., 2011. *Four Pillars of Destiny: A Guide to Relationships*, Bloomington (IN): iUniverse.

Kirousis, W., 2015. *Train your best today usac.*
Online. Available at:
http://www.slideshare.net/willkirousis/train-your-besttoday-usac-51120260 [Accessed 18th October 2015]

Lane, A. (2001) *'Relationship between perceptions of performance expectations and mood amongst distance runners'*, Journal of Science and Medicine in Sport, 4(1), 116-128.

Lyle, J., 2002. *Sports Coaching Concepts: A Framework for Coaches' Behaviour*. New York: Psychology Press.

Manz, C.C. (2000) *Emotional Discipline: The Power to Choose How You Feel*, San Francisco: Berrett-Koehler.

Markham, K.D., Klein, W.M.P. and Suhr, J.A (2008) *Handbook of Imagination and Mental Simulation, London*: Psychology Press.

May, R. (1975) *The Courage to Create*, New York: W.W.Norton.

Nicholls, A. R. & Jones, L., 2013. *Psychology in Sports Coaching: Theory and Practice*. London: Routledge.

Oliver, C., 2015. *The Philosophy of a Coach*. Online. Available at: http://www.slideshare.net/ChrisOliver6/the-philosophy-ofa-coach [Accessed 18th October 2015].

Orlick, T. (2000) *In Pursuit of Excellence: How to Win in Sport and Life Through Mental Training* (3rd Edition), Champaign, IL: Human Kinetics.

Pavlov, I., 1960. *Conditional Reflexes*. New York: Dover Publications.

Pill, S., 2008. *Teaching games for understanding*. Physical Education and Recreation, 29(2).

Potrac, P., Gilbert, W. & Deninson, J., 2013. *Routledge Handbook of Sports Coaching*. New York: Routledge.

Rotter, J. B., 1966. *Generalized expectancies for internal versus external control of reinforcement*. Psychological Monographs: General & Applied, 80(1), pp. 1-28.

Samah, A. et al., 2013. *Influence of coaches' behavior on athletes' motivation : Malaysian sport archery experience.* International Journal of Research in Management, 5(3), pp. 136-142.

Sheard, M. (2012) *Mental Toughness: The Mind-set Behind Sporting Achievement* (2nd Edition), London: Routledge.

Stafford, I., 2011. *Coaching Children in Sport*. London: Taylor & Francis.

Taylor, J & Wilson, G.S. (2005) *Applying Sport Psychology: Four Perspectives,* Champaign, IL: Human Kinetics.

White, A. A. K. (2009) *From Comfort Zone to Performance Management*, New York: White & MacLean Publishing.

CONTRIBUTORS

Alan Hinkes: World-leading mountaineer

Alan Hinkes (OBE) is one of only a handful of mountaineers to claim all 14 Himalayan 'eight-thousanders' (mountains above 8,000m in height), which he did on the 30 May 2005. He was awarded an OBE in the 2006 New Year Honours List for his achievements in mountaineering.

Alison Waters: World number three squash player

Alison Waters is a professional squash player. She reached number three in the world and has won team World and European Championships with England. She is also a Commonwealth silver medallist and British Champion.

Andy McMenemy: World-record breaking ultra-distance runner

In 2011, Andy McMenemy established a World Record by completing 66 Ultra Marathons in 66 consecutive days in the 66 official cities of the UK.

His tenacity, achievement and inspiration of other people has not gone un-noticed and Andy was honoured to receive The True Englishman of 2014 Award.

Before his ultra-marathon attempt, Andy successfully completed some of the world's toughest endurance races including the infamous Marathon des Sables and the Namibian Desert 24hr Ultra Marathon.

Ben Saunders: Record-breaking polar explorer

Ben Saunders is one of the world's leading polar explorers, and a record-breaking long-distance skier who has covered more than 7,000km (4,350 miles) on foot in the Polar Regions since 2001. His accomplishments include leading The Scott Expedition, the longest human-powered polar journey in history; the a 105-day expedition, from Ross Island on the coast of Antarctica to the South Pole and back again, that defeated Captain Scott and Sir Ernest Shackleton.

Ben is the third person in history to ski solo to the North Pole, and holds the record for the longest solo Arctic journey by a Briton. He is an ambassador for the Prince's Trust, a patron of British Exploring, and a fellow of the Royal Geographical Society.

Bruce Duncan: World-leading adventure racer
Bruce led Team GB to three consecutive victories in the Wenger Patagonian Expedition race. It is a 600 km tri-discipline race through the Chilean Andes, which is perhaps the most revered adventure race on Earth.

Chris Cook: double Olympian
Chris represented Team GB in the 50m, 100m and 200m breaststroke. He finished his career as a double Olympian, an Olympic finalist, double Commonwealth Champion, British and Commonwealth record holder and the seventh fastest man in history to swim the 100m breaststroke.

Chris Robertson: England Squash's national head coach
As a player, Chris reached number two in the world rankings and won team World Championships with Australia. He was appointed the Squash Wales national coach in 1994and England Head Coach of Squash and Racket Ball in 2011.

Kenny Atkinson: multiple Michelin-starred chef

Kenny has been awarded multiple Michelin stars, most recently at his own restaurant, 'House of Tides'. He also appeared on the BBC show Great British Menu, where he has twice taken a dish to the final banquet. In 2009, Kenny was named Chef of the Year at the 2009 Catey Awards.

WHAT'S NEXT?

You now have some practical principles, which can help you develop mental toughness. I genuinely hope that you find them valuable. If you found this little book useful, and would like to find out more, these might also be helpful.

To help your personal performance...

Two Lengths of the Pool

How to simplify, clarify and hone your focus, so that you can become as focused and effective as an Olympic athlete.

How to Shine

How ordinary people become world class. The eight key characteristics of world class performers, and how to develop them.

Could I Do That

How to take on massive, daunting and seemingly "impossible" challenges.

How to Develop Character

How to develop the characteristics you need to be successful.

Or to help develop teamwork and leadership...

Stronger Together

How to build a truly great team by adopting the characteristics of world class teams.

How to Herd Cats

How to lead a team of independent thinkers... who have their own opinions, self-interest and egos.

Search for these on Amazon, or wherever you buy your books.

I work with a huge variety of athletes, sports teams, leaders and organisations across the globe.

I help them conquer their challenges, achieve their potential, deliver their peak performance consistently and work towards becoming world class in their field.

If you'd like to discuss working together, please feel free to drop me a line. info@be-world-class.com

ABOUT THE AUTHOR

Simon Hartley is a globally respected sport psychology consultant and world-class performance coach. He helps athletes and business people throughout the world to get their mental game right.

For over 20 years, he has worked with gold medallists, world record holders, world champions, top five world ranked professional athletes, and multiple-championship winning teams.

Simon has worked at the highest level of sport, including spells in Premiership football, Premiership rugby union, First Class County Cricket, Super League, golf, tennis, motor sport and with Great British Olympians.

Since 2005, Simon has also applied the principles of sport psychology to business, education, healthcare and the charity sector. This has included projects with some of the world's leading corporations and foremost executives.

More recently, Simon has also become a highly acclaimed author and award-winning professional speaker.

For more information, please visit:

www.be-world-class.com

To find Simon's other books, please visit:

www.amazon.co.uk/Simon-Hartley/e/B005CERCJQ/

be world class

Printed in Great Britain
by Amazon